How to Open & O
Financially Suc

• • • • • • • • • • • • • • • •
Personal and Executive
Coaching Business
• • • • • • • • • • • • • • • •

With Companion CD-ROM

By Kristie Lorette
and John Peragine

How to Open & Operate a Financially Successful Personal and Executive Coaching Business: With Companion CD-ROM

Copyright © 2011 by Atlantic Publishing Group, Inc.
1405 SW 6th Ave. • Ocala, Florida 34471 • 800-814-1132 • 352-622-1875–Fax
Web site: www.atlantic-pub.com • E-mail: sales@atlantic-pub.com
SAN Number: 268-1250

Library of Congress Cataloging-in-Publication Data

Lorette, Kristie, 1975-
  How to open & operate a financially successful personal and executive coaching business : with companion CD-ROM / Kristie Lorette.
    p. cm.
  Includes bibliographical references and index.
  ISBN-13: 978-1-60138-227-6 (alk. paper)
  ISBN-10: 1-60138-227-8 (alk. paper)
  1. Personal coaching--Practice. 2. Executive coaching--Practice. 3. Counseling--Vocational guidance. I. Title. II. Title: How to open and operate a financially successful personal and executive coaching business.
  BF637.P36L67 2010
  658.3'124--dc22
                                    2008037166

PROJECT MANAGER: Sylvia Maye • PROOFREADER: Brad Goldbach
COVER DESIGN: Meg Buchner • megadesn@mchsi.com
BACK COVER DESIGN: Jackie Miller • millerjackiej@gmail.com

Printed on Recycled Paper

Printed in the United States

We recently lost our beloved pet "Bear," who was not only our best and dearest friend but also the "Vice President of Sunshine" here at Atlantic Publishing. He did not receive a salary but worked tirelessly 24 hours a day to please his parents.

Bear was a rescue dog that turned around and showered myself, my wife, Sherri, his grandparents Jean, Bob, and Nancy, and every person and animal he met (maybe not rabbits) with friendship and love. He made a lot of people smile every day.

We wanted you to know that a portion of the profits of this book will be donated to The Humane Society of the United States. *–Douglas & Sherri Brown*

The human-animal bond is as old as human history. We cherish our animal companions for their unconditional affection and acceptance. We feel a thrill when we glimpse wild creatures in their natural habitat or in our own backyard.

Unfortunately, the human-animal bond has at times been weakened. Humans have exploited some animal species to the point of extinction.

The Humane Society of the United States makes a difference in the lives of animals here at home and worldwide. The HSUS is dedicated to creating a world where our relationship with animals is guided by compassion. We seek a truly humane society in which animals are respected for their intrinsic value, and where the human-animal bond is strong.

Want to help animals? We have plenty of suggestions. Adopt a pet from a local shelter, join The Humane Society and be a part of our work to help companion animals and wildlife. You will be funding our educational, legislative, investigative and outreach projects in the U.S. and across the globe.

Or perhaps you'd like to make a memorial donation in honor of a pet, friend or relative? You can through our Kindred Spirits program. And if you'd like to contribute in a more structured way, our Planned Giving Office has suggestions about estate planning, annuities, and even gifts of stock that avoid capital gains taxes.

Maybe you have land that you would like to preserve as a lasting habitat for wildlife. Our Wildlife Land Trust can help you. Perhaps the land you want to share is a backyard— that's enough. Our Urban Wildlife Sanctuary Program will show you how to create a habitat for your wild neighbors.

So you see, it's easy to help animals. And The HSUS is here to help.

THE HUMANE SOCIETY
OF THE UNITED STATES.

2100 L Street NW • Washington, DC 20037 • 202-452-1100
www.hsus.org

Table of Contents

Chapter 3: Planning a Successful Leap into Coaching   77

Chapter 4: Putting Your Business Plan in Writing   103

Chapter 5: Setting Your Fees   121

Chapter 6: The Legalities of Starting Your Business   141

Chapter 7: Managing Revenue and Expenses   161

Chapter 8: How to Manage Your Time and Yourself 183

Chapter 9: Building Your Brand 201

Chapter 10: Finding Clients 221

Chapter 11: Client Interaction 239

Foreword

You are about to embark on a journey that will change your life! My own journey into the world of coaching began back in early 2002. The dot com bubble had burst, and I had been recently laid off from my corporate job. I had always wanted to start my own business, and now that I found myself unemployed, I had the perfect opportunity to go for it. However, like many people, I had no idea what kind of business I wanted to start. As I surveyed the landscape at the time, I remember noticing how many people were unhappy with some aspect of their life or business, and I thought there might be an opportunity. I came up with a concept that I could only describe as a "personal trainer for your life or business" and started talking to people about it. The idea seemed pretty well received, and after talking to a number of people, one of them said to me, "I have a friend that does something like that. She calls herself a 'Life Coach.'" I had never heard the term "Life Coach" before, and I could not wait to talk to her! Shortly after our conversation, I enrolled at Coach U, and thus began my journey into the world of coaching.

Eight years later, I've had the fortune of being able to assist hundreds of entrepreneurs, small business owners, corporate executives, and others to improve their businesses, as well as their lives. I feel blessed that I can do something I love, while adding tremendous value for others, and at the same time getting paid to do it. If you are the type of person that likes helping others, enjoys working with people, and has a unique expertise that you would like to share, then coaching may be a great fit for you. This book will help you figure that out.

I'll be the first one to tell you that coaching can be a very rewarding career. At the same time, it can be very challenging. Like any other business, coaching is a business, and a large percentage of people that get into the coaching profession do not experience the success they would like to enjoy. The great thing is, within these pages, the authors provide you with the tools that you will need to determine if the coaching business is the right business for you. Through her marketing expertise, she also shares with you the steps that you will need to take to create a successful coaching business, as well as a rewarding career as a coach. This great resource will assist you in getting off to a great start and help you avoid the common mistakes most people make as they enter into the field of coaching.

As you begin your journey, I encourage you to read through the book, do the exercises, and really consider the 'why' behind your interest in the coaching field. I truly believe that if you have a powerful reason why you want to do something, your passion will help you overcome the obstacles to your success. The best coaches that I know are role models for their clients, and are always challenging themselves to be a couple of steps ahead of them. If you enjoy developing yourself personally and becoming a role model for what is possible, I know you will be a great coach! When you combine your passion for helping others with the tools and techniques presented in this book, you will not only be a great coach, but you will also be successful in the coaching business. Here's to your success!

Tom Kelly, PCC
Professional Business Coach

*Tom Kelly is a successful business coach that specializes in working with small business owners, salespeople, entrepreneurs, and corporate executives. You can learn more about him at **www.businesscoachchicago.com**.*

Introduction

Deciding to become a business or life coach can be a life- and career-altering change in your personal and professional life. Reasons for becoming a coach can vary from person to person, but no matter what has pushed you toward taking this step, becoming a coach may just be the solution to all of your personal and career woes.

As a business or personal coach, you also have the power to control your own experiences and your destiny, which means you can alter your career and financial future. Imagine how empowered you feel as you set your own schedule, make your own decisions, and help clients answer questions and overcome the challenges that they cannot handle on their own. As a coach, you are the guiding force and can pull the answers from your own bank of knowledge and experience to help clients work through their own situations as effectively and productively as possible.

To become a successful coach, you must possess several primary qualities and characteristics including being a professional coach and have superior listening and analytical skills. You may very well have the skills and knowledge you need to launch a coaching business, but launching a business of any kind also requires that you have the skill set for running a business. Once you determine if starting your own coaching business is the right step for you, then you need the detailed instructions on how to make it happen.

HOW TO USE THIS BOOK

How to Open & Operate a Financially Successful Coaching Business includes everything you need to know to start your business venture off on the right path — and to continue driving the business on the road to success. The first part of the book provides you with the tools, resources, and self-assessments you need to evaluate your personal and financial situation. If the time is not right, this book helps you determine what you need to do to make it viable for you to start a coaching business. Once you get the timing to starting your business down, the rest of the book covers the various steps for establishing and running a financially successful coaching business.

Each chapter of the book covers what you need to know to build the foundation of each aspect of your business. From the different legal entity options for setting up the business (sole proprietorship or corporation) to marketing your business and handling clients, you will learn all of the things you need to know and be aware of how to create as successful a coaching business as possible.

The beginning of each chapter includes a bullet point list as a preview of the topics covered in the upcoming chapter. This sets your expectations for what information you will walk away with once you have completed the chapter. Scattered throughout the chapter you will find checklists, tips, and warnings directly related to the topic at hand. There is no reason for you to reinvent the wheel and make the same mistakes those coaches who came before you have made. Heeding these warnings and using the advice provided streamlines the process for you so you can avoid making the same common mistakes that many new coaches make.

Keep an open mind as you read through the next 12 chapters. While owning your own business means you are your own boss, you still have to be accountable for your actions to be successful. Knowledge is power, and if you take what you learn from this book and apply it to your business then you are sure to create a powerful business. You are reading this book because you have an interest in becoming a coach, so soak up all of the information you can so it winds up being a positive venture. Financial and personal situations, objectives, and goals vary from person to person, so you will need to mold and adjust the advice to fit your particular situation. Use the information in this book to learn the benefits and disadvantages for each aspect of the coaching business world. Then, use this information to make a personal decision for what is the right option for you.

Chapter 1:
Timing Your Start

In this chapter, you will:

- Learn the top reasons individuals become coaches and determine your own reasons for seeking a coaching career.

- Determine if the timing is right to launch your coaching business.

- Uncover and analyze the personal, professional, and financial considerations of starting and running a coaching business.

- Conduct a self-assessment to determine if coaching is the right career for you.

There is a misconception that a coach is someone who provides expert advice and guidance in exchange for a fee, but in actuality, a coach is a person who offers options for which the client should consider. A coach is not a consultant — a person hired to provide expert advice based on their area of expertise. It is important, as you begin your journey to opening your own coaching business, that you understand the distinction.

The great thing about coaches is that coaching options are as varied as the choices on a restaurant's food menu. Coaches come from different backgrounds, live in different areas, have different work experiences, and can range from the working with individuals in a specific industry to coaches who work with a specific type of client or a generalist who helps individuals tackle personal or professional challenges. If you had to boil coaching down to one word, limitless is a possibility.

Before you start the process of launching your own business, stop and ask yourself one basic question: Why do you want to become a coach? For many would-be coaches, the answer to this question is freedom. Most individuals who venture out on their own to open a business do it because they want to be their own boss, make their own hours, and do what they want without having to answer to a boss. Being a coach provides you with this type of freedom.

REASONS TO BE A COACH

Take a look at some of the common reasons people choose to become coaches and see if your reason or reasons are the same. This section covers some of the common reasons coaches make their way into the coaching business, but if your reason is not listed here, it does not mean that you are not ready to become a coach or you should not do it. Make sure you consider your own reasons and how becoming a coach would benefit you.

Use your expertise

Everyone has an area of expertise they are passionate about, whether it is dogs, marketing, or streamlining a manufacturing process. One of the top reasons people become coaches is to use a talent currently being stifled in their career, and they are ready to unleash and finally put that talent to good use. For some, their area of expertise is a hobby or more of a personal interest than that of a professional nature, but by no means does this mean that you should rule it out as a coaching option.

If you have worked as a restaurant manager for the last 20 years, then it is probably safe to say that no one knows the ins and outs of the restaurant business better than you do. Rather than continue to manage the restaurant, why not spread your wealth of knowledge to a greater number of restaurants — helping to coach restaurant owners to make the most of their own restaurant businesses and careers, make productive decisions about their restaurant business, streamline the serving process, create superior customer experiences, and boost the bottom lines. Or maybe you have worked in marketing in various roles and for various companies. Over the past 15 years, you have seen what works when it comes to creating, implementing, and tracking marketing campaigns. You eat, sleep, and breathe marketing. You have the keen ability to look at a company's offerings and create a strategic marketing plan that can help them sell and increase revenues like there is no tomorrow. You can apply this talent, share it with numerous companies, and make money doing it by helping to mold, coach, and guide business owners in their marketing efforts or marketing professionals in their careers.

Consider what areas of expertise you have and determine whether there is a market that has needs you can fulfill. Will someone pay you to help them overcome their career fears? Will someone pay you to teach him or her how to overcome personal challenge that is holding him or her back in all areas of life? Will someone pay you to coach them as a business owner to implement that marketing plan that has been sitting on their desk for the past three months? If the answer to your question is yes, then there may be a need you can fulfill in the market and make money doing it in the process.

Laid off and unemployed

Especially since the economy's downturn that started in 2007, layoffs and unemployment are a reality for many employees of companies — especially employees that have been around for multiple years. When companies downsize, it is often the highest-paid (and most-experienced) individuals who get cut first because it helps companies cut costs quickly and easily. In fact, many of the individuals who get laid off might have been contemplating forging out on their own for years and joining the ranks of the unemployed may be the reason they needed to break out on their own and finally open the business they have been yearning for.

If being laid off from your job is staring you in the face, or if you have recently found yourself unemployed, you may be able to find safety and security as a coach. In today's ever-changing economy, almost any type and size business can terminate its employees without advanced notice or a severance package. Becoming a coach can be the solution to this problem for you. In fact, when you become a coach, you get to choose who you work with as clients just as much as your clients choose to work with you. You may even be the one firing clients rather than the other way around. In many situations, you earn more money as a coach than working as an employee for a company. Not only does coaching eliminate the unemployment factor, but it also can increase your level of income.

Be the boss

Becoming a coach is not only about venturing into a new career. It is also about becoming a business owner. So, one of the top reasons why individuals turn to coaching work instead of working as an employee is that they are tired of applying their talent and skills to make money for someone else. Coaching allows you to use your skills and talent to turn a profit for yourself and for your family.

Being your own boss allows you to make your own decisions. From working the schedule you want (even if it is in the middle of the night) to removing the cap from your potential income, being your own boss puts you in control of your career. Not having to answer to someone else on a daily basis removes many of the constraints that hold a typical employee back from reaching the peak of his or her success. Becoming a coach positions you to earn your own profits and create your own destiny.

Creates more income

Even those who wish to continue working a full-time or part-time job can become a coach to generate additional income. Coaching allows you to set your own schedule, work around your other engagements, and continue working at your full-time position. In addition, you can work where and when you want to — even if it is at 3 a.m. sitting up in bed in your pajamas.

Getting past the glass ceiling

Every company has a limit on how high you can reach as an employee. Even if your final position with a company is president and CEO, you cannot go any higher than this position. No matter how hard you work and how many hours you put in, there is a limit on how far you can go with a company. Because you are in control of everything from how many hours you put in to how much you charge a client, your income and your goals can reach way beyond the confines of a typical company infrastructure if you choose to open your own coaching business.

TIMING YOUR MOVE

From what is going on in the economy to what is going on in your personal and professional life, there are factors to timing your transition from your current employment situation into the world of coaching. Though there is no conclusive test that provides a flashing sign that says the time is now, you need to assess all of the personal, financial, and experiential aspects of your personal situation as you work your way through the decision-making process.

Professional considerations

There is no rule that says you cannot love what you do as a career. In fact, working as a coach probably requires you to love what you do more because you are the owner of the business, as well as the employee. Coaching will be your career, so the first thing you need to consider is your professional situation. If you want to be a successful coach, you have to have the skills, resources, and experience required to perform the job you are signing on to do.

You need to possess a unique selling proposition (USP), a benefit or a reason for companies or individuals to want and need to hire you as a coach. For example, if your full-time career has been in the automotive industry, but you want to kick off your professional coaching career in coaching marketing professionals, you have to have the expertise in marketing and understanding the inner workings of the marketing profession to make it happen. It is important that you be realistic when you are assessing your move into the world of coaching. A solid foundation of experience is essential to launching and maintaining a successful coaching career, but here are some other items to consider and evaluate.

People skills

Beyond being a subject expert or knowing how to work with a particular type of person or profession, being a professional coach also requires that you have an advanced set of people skills and a huge amount of patience. Coaching is a business where you are constantly working with individuals or groups of people on a face-to-face or phone basis. Practically every aspect of being a coach involves directly working with your clients. If you dislike working with people or are more of an independent worker than a counselor or guide, then the coaching business is probably not the right line of work for you.

Degrees, licensing, or certifications

In some professions, a license, degree, or related certifications can be an important factor. These pieces of paper can add value to your services as a coach and may make the difference of being hired or being passed over for a coaching opportunity. Licenses, certifications, and degrees are proof of your expert-level of experience and knowledge. Some professions require these items by law, but other professions can use it to their advantage to charge more money or convince a client to hire them. *Chapter 6 covers more of the legalities of licenses and other legal steps you may need to take to become a coach and to open your coaching business.* You can also update and refresh your skills with continuing education classes and courses.

Certification also provides you with credibility because certification programs require rigorous training, so working your way through a certification program provides you with the backing from an accredited organization. *For a list of certification programs, see Appendix A.*

Certification by a reputable coaching organization, such as the International Coaching Federation (ICF), is important both as a way to keep your skills sharp and as a way of making coaching a more reputable and credentialed profession. Each coach should decide whether certification is the best route for him or her. Here are some ideas to keep in mind:

- In most cases, the general public has no idea what coaching professional organizations are or about the importance of certification.

- It is important to be a member of an organization, such as the ICF, and to commit to the code of ethics of the organization. It is important to promote that you are a committed member of the organization to your clients to establish your credibility. Making your clients aware of your credentials also enables them to file a complaint with the organization if they feel you have breached the code of ethics.

- If you choose to obtain certification, you have to do the work to get clients to know how important this process is, and that it is what sets you apart from your competition. The coaching organization that awards you the certification may or may not be doing much promotion to the general public. You can take responsibility for your own promotion by highlighting your expertise and certification in your marketing materials.

- The coaching industry does not self-regulate as efficiently as other industries do, and there are no governing bodies to enforce ethical and professional issues. Therefore, being certified by an outside organization is totally voluntary.

- Getting your credentials can be financially beneficial, as well as emotionally satisfying. The real question is, "Which professional body do I want to obtain certification from?" Review the previous points with this frame of mind. The ICF is the world's biggest and most recognized coaching body, but that does not necessarily make them the best. You may want to consider getting certified with more than one organization.

- Consider what the requirements are for maintaining your certification. Some organizations have robust requirements, while others simply require you to pay a fee each year. Beware of organizations that require you to jump through hoops that you may consider unethical or inappropriate, so ask questions about policies before choosing a certification organization.

Because many states do not regulate coaching, certification adds credibility. It is through many of these organizational databases that people connect with coaches, thus making certification and accreditation organizations a great resource for building your business.

If you type any combination of words into an Internet search engine, such as "coaching," "life coaching," "executive coaching," or any other words to describe coaching, you will see listings for a number of certification agencies. These can vary in price and offerings, so look closely before committing to any particular coaching school. Look at how long the organizations have been around and check the organization using the Better Business Bureau at **www.bbb.com**. You can type in the name of the business and see if there are any complaints. Ask other coaches where they were certified, and see what they know about the various programs available.

Next, consider whether you have the professional references to back up your claim that you can be the coach your clients need. References provide a list of customers or professionals who can vouch for the quality of the work you provide to land new clients on a continuous basis. This list is also a starting point for your coaching work because these individuals may be willing to hire you to fulfill their own needs. Past customers can also be valuable resources for referrals for new business.

Becoming a coach and running your own coaching business also requires that you have some level of knowledge on how to run a business. Not only do you have to have the acumen to work as a coach, but you also have to be able to wear all of the hats required for running a business. The business sides of coaching means having the ability to write and follow a business plan, hire a staff, run the office, pay taxes, and more. If you have never run a business before these are things you can learn in this book right along with learning how to be a coach.

Financial considerations

When it comes to your financial situation, there is a fine line between your personal finances and the financial aspect of running a business. Financially, you must have the cash on hand to pay for the start-up and operational costs of running the business, but you also need to make sure you have enough money to pay your living expenses while you are getting the business up and running. Remember that the majority of businesses do not start to turn a profit until after the first one or two years in business. For some businesses, it is even longer. You have to have access to a pool of money to cover you financially until the business starts paying for itself and starts paying you a salary.

Financial constraints are probably the largest deterrent for individuals looking to start a career as a coach. They may be making a satisfactory income in their current position as an employee, not have enough savings to give up this current income, or lack the ambition or motivation to shoulder the risk of starting a new business. Most business experts suggest you have enough money in cash reserves to cover your personal and business expenses for at least six months to a year.

If you do not currently have this amount of cash reserves, then you may need to save some additional money before launching your coaching business. Another option is to look to other sources such as a small business loan or borrowing money from a friend or family member to cover the costs of starting the business. Here are some ways you can prepare financially for your transition to being the owner of a coaching business:

Beef up your savings account

Start planning your coaching career by putting away as much money as possible before jumping in with both feet. Save as much as possible to provide a bigger safety net to cover both regular and emergency expenses. Take a look at the balance of your savings account. If you are currently living from paycheck to paycheck, now may not be time to become a full-time coach. If you have funds that can be easily liquidated such as stocks, bonds, mutual funds, or other assets, then you may have the safety net you need to fall back on until your business starts turning a profit.

Income and assets to cover expenses

Create a list of personal and expected business expenses, then see how many months or years the balance of cash you have will cover your expenses. Is your current after-tax income covering your current expenses? Do you have money you can pull from to cover these expenses if your income fluctuates or changes as you transition into coaching? If not, you may want to consider saving additional money or working as a part-time coach until you can get your financial situation on steady ground. Starting a new career and business is stressful enough without having to add the stress of being financially unstable. Start off on financially stable ground so that if your coaching income is not enough to pay your expenses, you have options to fall back on until you can take on more clients, charge more for your services, or find a way to reduce your expenses.

Protect your future

Even as your business starts to take off, there are going to be financial good times and financial bad times. It is important to plan for the less-than-optimal times when you may not have enough clients or be generating enough revenue in your business to cover expenses. When times are good in your business, make sure to put away money for unexpected expenses or tougher times. If there is a large, unexpected expense, this ensures you have funds to keep your business afloat until the good times come back around again. If your office bathroom springs a leak and floods your entire office (and you do not have insurance to cover this type of catastrophe), you may have to pay to clean up the water and replace any equipment, furniture, flooring, walls and other items damaged in the flood.

Chapter 7 goes into more detail about how to estimate your business expenses and how much you need to have to launch and keep your business afloat until it is self-sufficient. Right now, it is essential to consider where you need to start to assess whether now is the right time to launch the business or if a little more preparation is in order first.

Personal considerations

Starting a business, especially a coaching business, has a personal side to it. Being a coach is a service-based business, which means you are going to be working directly with your clients, either face-to-face or by phone. It is slightly different from a product-based business where you are selling an item manufactured by someone else.

On top of the personal side of business, starting a small business requires a lot of personal dedication and commitment to start small and grow into a larger, profit-making machine. Launching and maintaining a business can take a personal toll on you and your family. Addressing the concern that launching your coaching business may and probably is going to take time away from your personal time right now helps you to prepare and decide if a coaching business is the right choice for you.

Seek advice from others

Talk with your spouse, children, other family members, and friends to see what their opinions are on starting your business. Analyzing the launch of your coaching career from all of the different angles can help make the difference between succeeding and failing. You may also want to spend time talking with people you know who started their own businesses and even reach out to other coaches. One place you may be able to meet and mingle with other coaches is by attending a professional coaching association meeting. Check your local area for groups that cater to the coaching business.

Personal lifestyle

If you work during the traditional office hours of 9 a.m. to 5 p.m. and have weekends off, this schedule can be turned upside down when you become a coach. You will have clients and situations where you have to work on the weekends or field a client call at midnight on a Friday (although this may be rare) or have to leave your child's school play because there is an emergency situation you have to help a client overcome. The essence is that the line between your personal life and your work life becomes blurred.

Motivation level

One of the biggest personal characteristics a coach must possess is self-motivation, especially when you first start your business, because you may be the one and only employee. This means there is not a manager peering over your shoulder to make sure that you are doing everything you are supposed to be doing. You have to be able to manage yourself, set your schedule, meet deadlines, juggle clients, and set and meet goals all on your own. Some people can thrive and survive in this type of environment while others need a more structured work environment. You have to know yourself and assess your ability to manage yourself in order to excel in a coaching career. If you struggle with keeping yourself on task and motivated to accomplish your goals, then you may struggle with starting and running your own business.

CASE STUDY: THE DECISION TO START COACHING

Eva Gregory
Leading Edge Coaching & Training
P O Box 99656 Emeryville, CA 94662
Phone: 510.597.0687 * Fax: 510.588.5477
www.coacheva.com

The decision to start coaching for Eva Gregory was not a difficult one, as she spent years in the computer industry and finally became burned out due to stress. "I decided to get out of "hi-tech" and into "high people." After studying metaphysics for over a decade and with a keen interest in personal growth and person growth development, I thought I would be doing personal growth workshops," she said.

Gregory specializes in empowering individuals and organizations to produce outstanding results through the use of individual coaching, group coaching, teleclasses, and workshops. She also empowers her clients, not only in their business lives, but in their personal lives as well. "My unwavering belief is that all of us have the power to change anything in our lives and design it purposefully!" Gregory said.

For new coaches, worrying about how much you do not know is pointless. It is more important to focus on what you can learn. "Find a school that fits the type of coaching you want to do, and that fits your lifestyle. For instance, do you prefer to work over the phone or do you prefer to have face-to-face training? I did not have a business card, website, or anything that marketed me when I started out," she said. "After my first conversation with my first coach from a Toastmasters Conference, I signed up right away." Another piece of advice when you finally make the decision to coach is to start where you are. Gregory said you should begin coaching right away — even if it is for free. You can even call it on-the-job training. Gregory believes it is through the experience of actually doing it where you will find the real learning.

When Gregory did her first two-day workshop, what she felt afterward helped her affirm and assess her career choice. "I felt like I had empty nest syndrome."

"What happened to these folks? How were their lives impacted? What did they do with what they had learned? I knew I wanted more ongoing, although I did not know what that would be," she said. Two weeks later, Gregory attended a Toastmasters Conference and in the first breakout session she attended, the speaker talked about a profession called life coaching. She said had never heard of it, but as she began to listen closer; she had an epiphany and knew what was finally missing. "I called him up that night and said, 'I want to be what you are when I grow up and I want you to be my coach,'" said Gregory.

Two months later, she was in her first training weekend with the Coaches Training Institute where she received her certification and she said that she could not be happier doing what she loves. "I've been on my honeymoon with this profession ever since," she said.

Eva Gregory, known as America's FeelGood Coach™, is a speaker and author of several programs and books including The Feel Good Guide to Prosperity, The Prosperity Game Home Study Course™, The Magnetizing Money Course™, Law of Attraction Hot Topics!™ and 12 Weeks to Financial Fortune™.

IS THERE A NEED YOU CAN FILL?

Nearly 600,000 new small businesses open each year, but that does not mean all 600,000 are going to reel in profits. According to the National

Federation of Independent Business (NFBI), 39 percent of these businesses are profitable, 30 percent break even, and 30 percent lose money — 1 percent falls in the "unable to determine" category. With a multitude of mitigating factors, determining the success or failure rate of these companies, there is not a litmus test you can take to see if your business will fall in the success or failure pile. Removing everything else from the equation, you need to ask yourself one important question: Is my coaching business marketable?

One of the biggest ways to ensure success is to make sure your coaching business has a market of customers ready and willing to buy your services. No matter how great you think your idea is, if there is not an audience of paying customers to hire you then you will quickly go down in flames. Rather than try to create a market for your business, create your business to fill the need of a particular market. Think long and hard about who your potential clients are. What groups of businesses, organizations, or individuals need the coaching services you are thinking of providing? Literally sit down with a pen and paper in hand and create a list of broad categories of potential clients. Then start to narrow down potential clients using trade publications, phone books, the Internet, and working through your network of contacts to get more specific on who these potential clients are, how they think, how they act, and anything else you can determine their thoughts and behaviors.

Finally, do some quick competitive research. See if there are coaches out in the world offering services that fit the needs of the potential clients you have gathered information from and on. The truth of the matter is that there probably is at least one other coach out there offering the service you are thinking of providing. Even if there are several coaches offering the same service, there is something unique about you and your service offering that sets you apart from the competition. Determine what this innovative item is, write it down, and set it aside for now. You will need this information later when it comes time to write your business and marketing plan. Keep in mind that choosing a coach often comes down to a feel of comfort between you and your client. Clients choose personal and professional coaches that they feel comfortable working with.

Doing work you love can be personally rewarding, but it is also important to determine if doing what you love can be profitable. Though it may take one or two years for your coaching business to start turning a profit, the business has to have the ability to turn a profit in the long run in order for it to be prosperous. When researching your competition, see what fees they are charging. Use these fees in conjunction with your potential client list to calculate an estimate of revenues for your business. Start out with conservative figures and estimate monthly, quarterly, and annual income. Take into consideration that the first few years are going to be slower than later years, but put some realistic facts and figures down on paper. A good place to start is with your current income. If your current annual income is $75,000, set the goal for your first year in business at the same number and work backwards to figure out if this is a realistic goal for the business.

Then you have to ask yourself the million-dollar question: Can the business generate enough in revenues to cover and eventually exceed expenses?

The economic turn of events

Starting in 2007 and continuing through 2010, a downturn in the economy has had a direct effect on the timing of starting a coaching business. As more and more companies are forced to close their doors or downsize, an unprecedented number of people are unemployed and without many options for future employment. When times are tough, it may be next to impossible to find a company to hire you.

This is where starting a coaching business using your skills and expertise can come in handy.

Even in hard times, businesses need individuals to perform tasks that keep the business running and profitable. Tough times also propel individuals to spend their disposable income on items that make them feel good, so spas, nail and hair salons, and even personal coaches all tend to see an increase in their business.

So even though the job market itself may look bleak with companies cutting back budgets, laying off employees, or closing their doors forever, these situations may be creating opportunities for coaching businesses — making it a prime time to get your business up and running. On the other hand, more stringent lending guidelines have made it harder for individuals and small businesses to obtain new credit and loans. This means that it may be difficult for you to borrow or find the seed money you need to pay for your startup costs, making it more important than ever to make sure you have your finances in order before you decide to start your coaching firm.

IS COACHING RIGHT FOR YOU?

Coaching is a type of career that people seem to have a calling to perform. Individuals attracted to a coaching career typically feel drawn to unselfishly helping others. They find great joy in seeing those they work with succeed — the greater the accomplishment that is achieved, the greater the reward for the coach. Many professional coaches concur that it was their most difficult cases that they remember more clearly because of the excitement that both they and the client experienced when finally overcoming hurdles. If you are the type of person that feels propelled toward making people's lives more joyful and complete, then coaching may be the right career path for you, so read on.

WHY COACHING AND NOT SOME OTHER WAY OF HELPING PEOPLE

Coaches come from many different paths to help people achieve goals in many different ways. Some are former therapists looking for a different way to help people, where they can apply the tools and techniques they learned as a therapist in new and dynamic ways. Therapists turned coaches are not dealing with pathology, but rather with potential. By using techniques such as active listening and reframing and skills such as compassion and people skills it takes to build positive rapport with their clients, coaches can have breakthroughs with clients that a therapist may not be able to achieve.

Coaching tends to be more of a fluid and dynamic profession than other professions that deal with helping others because it offers clients the freedom of choice they did not even know existed before working with a coach. Coaching professionals tend to be those who enjoy a different, more dynamic way of helping people by guiding clients in the right direction and creating what is usually a happy ending (which is not always the case in a traditional therapy scenario).

In essence, coaches fulfill a role that a therapist simply could not. For example, it would seem out of place for an executive of a large company, such as Yahoo!, to walk into a therapist's office and say, "I want to know how to manage my employees better, reduce conflict at work, and increase morale."

A typical therapist may respond by saying, "OK. Well, what problems are you experiencing?" The executive may respond with "No problems per se — I just need weekly support and guidance on how to be a better executive and boss. I want to eventually move up in the company and need help creating a business plan for myself."

This is where an executive or a personal coach is a more suited role for accomplishing this task than a therapist.

THE PROS AND CONS OF COACHING

As is the case with any career choice, there are pros and cons of coaching. There are things you will like and things you will dislike. It is up to you to make an informed decision whether coaching is the career for you by doing your homework ahead of time, so it saves you from disappointment and grief later. Use the following list to learn about some of the pros and cons of being a coach to see how it may apply to your own personal situation:

THE PROS AND CONS OF COACHING	
+ Pros	**- Cons**
You can provide a place of support that is unique and allows for significant life changes. Clients who have been stuck for years in life situations, such as bad relationships or being passed over for work promotions, find movement for the first time when working with a coach.	Coaches do not work with pathologies, but a good coach will recognize there is a problem and send them to the appropriate professional. Mental health issues can be frustrating for a coach, as they stunt the client's progress.
You help your client achieve their goals much quicker than other services can or by tackling the issue alone. You can also help the client make internal changes more quickly.	Sometimes a client only presents one aspect of the issue, which limits the ability of the coach to see the whole picture. The coach is only as good as the client allows himself to be seen. This can significantly slow down the coaching process and the ability to elicit change in the client's life.

THE PROS AND CONS OF COACHING

You can reach your clients in a much more powerful way than you can in other types of work, and you can take a deeper look into their lives.	Sometimes coaches or clients do not go deep enough and only deal with surface issues, which stunts change and progress, making coaching goals unattainable.
Coaching offers a variety of strategies to fit different clients' needs and learning styles. Coaches can tailor their approach in a way that recognizes each client's individuality and unique strengths and weaknesses. This takes some work and assessment on the coach's part because the outcome is based on an individual approach for each client.	Coaches are not therapists, so they may not know why a client acts a certain way. A coach only knows what the client is dealing with, what the client wants, and how to help the client achieve it. Though knowing those things is important, it still may not be enough to help a client reach his or her objectives.
Coaching is short-term. A coach can provide quick, effective support with immediate and sustained results. The interventions by a coach can be as short as a couple of months; this is because the coach can work with their clients a few days a week and offer support in between sessions. A coach creates their credibility through the results of their interventions with their clients.	Because there is no legal regulation of coaching in most states, anyone can claim to be a coach. Many organizations provide certifications, but these trainings are not mandated. A coach has to prove his or her worth to clients that may have had a bad experience with a coach who had less training or ability.
The work environment is flexible so you may find yourself working from home, a coffee shop, or the beach. A coach can choose where and when to conduct business; although it should be somewhere private and without distractions.	It can be financially difficult for a coach when starting a coaching business because a regular client base needs to be established to coach full-time. Many coaches need to start off part-time, rather than quitting their full-time jobs.

THE PROS AND CONS OF COACHING

A coach does not have to work the traditional office hours — they can make appointments with clients when it is convenient for them. There is a certain amount of flexibility in establishing office hours for international coaches due to time zone differences.	You do not have the one-on-one interaction with people over the phone or Internet as you would in person. It is sometimes hard to judge clients' reactions and level of understanding during a phone conversation.
High income potential — virtually limitless — with some coaches making more than $100,000 a year. If a coach can tap into the right market and build a decent reputation, he or she can live comfortably.	You have to use proper money management to have money from the profitable times to cover slow or not so profitable time in business.
You get to do something that you are passionate about and can help people change their lives. There is a great emotional satisfaction that comes with seeing a client make progress and positive changes in their life.	There may be a lot of competition. You may struggle if you do not choose the right market or method of delivery for your services.
You are your own boss. You decide how your business is run, and when you need time off, you make can make that decision on your own.	You are your own boss. There is no one to turn to when there are important and tough decisions to make.

THE PROS AND CONS OF COACHING

Coaches can take trips when they want, and get to work with creative people all around the world. They can learn and be exposed to a number of different cultures and, in some cases, can take expenses-paid trips to work with clients one-on-one.	Coaches have to do their own taxes and accounting — they must learn to manage their money responsibility and learn all of the tax laws and regulations or outsource it to an affordable professional. There are no built-in benefits, such as insurance, expense accounts or retirement plans. Any benefits have to be purchased directly by the coaching business.
You can increase your own personal growth by helping others and learning along the way.	Dealing with client issues and difficulties can be overwhelming at times. You are not going to get along with every client, and some will stretch your patience and objectivity.
You can find and maintain life-long positive and supportive relationships.	You cannot help everyone. This can be frustrating at times when you pour your heart into it and the clients do not achieve their goals.
If you decide to move past coaching at some point, you will have built a network and gained powerful experience that can help launch you into many other successful careers.	If you are a coach for a number of years it can lock you into a career path that may make it difficult to be reinserted in a traditional workforce.
You will be appreciated for what you do. Having positive feedback is more powerful than dollars in the bank. Coaching will boost and uplift your spirit and confidence.	If a client is dissatisfied with your work, they can spread negative feedback to potential future clients. It is difficult to make everyone happy all of the time.

Everyone possesses an internal basket — a basket that contains the vital energy humans need to feel alive. Although some of these needs come from biological processes, others come from less of a scientific place.

Sometimes a person's basket feels full and sometimes it feels empty. When someone is happy — laughing and joyful — it fills the internal basket. Love, passion, compassion, and other positive emotions also fill the basket. The basket can also become empty from feelings of hate, jealousy, discontent, rage, and other negative thoughts and emotions.

A coach gives of their essence to help motivate and move forward the clients who feel as if their emotional basket is empty or is starting to empty out. In fact, many personal and business coaches have coaches of their own to help them keep their own emotional baskets full. A coach with a full basket is able to give more of themselves and better help their clients fill up their own baskets.

CHECKLIST

- ✓ List your reason(s) for wanting to turn into a coach.

- ✓ Analyze the personal, professional, and financial considerations of starting and running a coaching business and make sure everything is in order.

- ✓ Assess the pros and cons of becoming a coach and see which side weighs heavier.

Chapter 2:
What Type of
Coach Are You?

In this chapter, you will:

- Decide what type of coach you want to be.

- Assess your personal and financial situation to help you make your coaching type choice.

- Discover the various types of coaches and some of the industries coaches serve.

- See what coaches do (services, products, and advice they offer clients).

- Observe a "day-in-the-life" look at what being a coach is like.

- Learn some of the pitfalls a coach faces when working with clients.

- Learn suggestions on how to avoid making these same mistakes.

Now that you know coaching is the right career move for you, it is time to start dealing with the details of becoming a coach. Coaching is not a one-size-fits-all career. It is a career position that has some flexibility built into it as far as how to set it up. Some coaches operate their business on the side while they continue to work a full-time job. Others solely have the intention of working as a coach on a part-time basis to generate additional income. The final set of coaches operate on a full-time basis where coaching is their only line of work and main source of income.

How you establish and run your coaching business has everything to do with your personal, professional, and financial situation. For example, if you are the sole breadwinner and provider for your family, it may not be a viable option to quit your day job and launch a new business. Instead, you may have to launch your coaching business in steps, while continuing to work full-time and run your coaching business on a part-time basis. As your business grows and you start turning a profit adequate enough to cover your personal and business expenses, then you can phase out your role as the employee for another company and phase in coaching on a full-time basis.

Another popular option for those who wish to work as a coach but are not yet ready to launch their own business is to land a coaching position with an established coaching firm. This allows you to work in the coaching field, enjoy some of the flexibility of working as a coach, and to earn the income a coach can pull in without having the headache of being a business owner at the same time. Working for a coaching firm has its advantages because you typically earn a salary and receive employee benefits such as health insurance and a retirement plan. You may also benefit because there is a set of established clients for you to work with or you may be expected to find your own clients. If you have not worked as a coach before, working for an established firm may set the stage for you to go out on your own later. You can learn a lot from working for a coaching firm — skills and ideas that you can modify and use to launch your own business when the time is right. This approach allows you to take a slower and more direct route to opening your own coaching business.

COACH INDUSTRIES

One of the best things about choosing a career as a coach is you can consult on almost anything for any type of consumer, business, or organization. When people think of coaches, they generally think of a counselor, psychiatrist or psychologist. In reality, coaches do tend to have some similar characteristics to these professions, but professional coaches also serve a variety or companies, consumers, for-profit and nonprofit organizations, government agencies, schools, and more.

Although some coaches cater to a particular type of business entity, most choose to narrow their service offering down even further. How specific a coach gets is totally up to them: You may find a coach that specializes in working with professional women that work in the finance field in the state of Florida. The more highly specialized a coach is, the smaller the pool of potential clients usually is. On the flipside, the more highly specialized a coach is, the higher the fee typically is for the coach's services because clients with a specific need are willing to pay a premium to work with a coach with the experience that fits that need.

You may think being more of a generalist when it comes to coaching is better, but many clients prefer to work with someone who is a specialist. When you specialize in a certain area, you are positioned as an expert in your field, become a valuable commodity to the client, and can warrant a higher fee because clients are willing to pay more for top performers like you.

EXECUTIVE COACHING	
Type of Coaching	**Considerations**
Executive Coaching	Most of this book is dedicated to successful executive coaching. Obtaining coaching certification, experience, and/or a degree working in business can also be beneficial.
Managers	Having experience working as a manager can help you succeed in coaching managers. Obtaining coaching certification, experience and/or a degree working in business can also be beneficial.
Fortune 500 companies	Experience working with or in one or more Fortune 500 companies or work as an executive for a large, successful company.
Human resource management	Having a degree in human resources or working as a human resources manager.
Corporate management	Working as an executive at a company and/or having a business degree.
Women in management	Being a woman might help attract other women to your coaching business, especially if you want to coach in this area. Being a strong role model can be important in coaching, as it helps to create credibility and portray an understanding of what other women are going through.

EXECUTIVE COACHING	
Men in management	Most men do not need a male coach to identify with their needs, so you can specialize in coaching men whether you are a man or a woman.
Management relations coach	A degree in business or business management and/or experience in one or more management position(s).
Management training coach	Experience working as a trainer in companies or as a coach in another related field may be helpful.

MARKETING INDUSTRY	
Type of Coaching	**Considerations**
Marketing Industry	Those with a background in marketing are typically successful in this niche.
Marketing expert coach	Experience working with various aspects of online and offline marketing. Overall knowledge of the marketing industry, marketing strategies and the latest in trends, as well as basic marketing tactics. Strategic marketing, joint ventures, affiliate marketing, and search engine optimization (SEO) are a few areas you need to have knowledge and experience working.
Retail coach	Retail sales and management experience and knowledge. Retail coaches can help clients improve sales and be a more effective sales people.

MARKETING INDUSTRY	
Advertising	Advertising is a subset of marketing, where coaches work with advertising professionals to develop skills to increase the client base and produce more dynamic advertising campaigns.
Gender-based marketing	This niche works with marketers that are targeting specific genders in their advertising. Women's studies, psychology, and experience working in marketing for gender-based products and services can be beneficial in a successful coaching career.
Marketing managers	A business degree or a business management degree may help coaches in this niche as it combines marketing and business management. Experience and knowledge in marketing, both big picture and detail-oriented marketing strategies, and tactics are necessary to succeed.
Public relations	A degree in public relations or a degree in public administration may help a coach in this niche, and, of course, experience in public relations would be necessary to target the clients in this niche.

SMALL BUSINESSES	
Type of Coaching	**Considerations**
Small Businesses	With many different aspects of running a small business, a coach that specializes in coaching small business owners can focus on overall small business management or specialize in one aspect of the business (i.e., marketing). Experience working as a small business owner or with small business owners is necessary as small business needs are very different than big business need. Experience running a successful small business, or a business degree can be helpful in this niche.
Start-up business owners	Experience starting your own small business or helping other business owners to get their businesses off the ground. A business degree is helpful for coaching in this niche.
Home-based business owners	Experience working as a home-based business owner or employee. Experience and knowledge of zoning laws, setting up a home office, record keeping and the challenges a home-based business owner faces.
Coaches	Experience as a trainer or educator or even a degree in or experience working in psychology can be helpful to work in this niche. You can use this book as a guide in working with your clients.

SMALL BUSINESSES	
Specialty businesses, such as wedding consultants or personal trainers	Knowledge or experience working in the type of small business you are coaching in (i.e., wedding consulting or personal training).
Partnership building	Experience and knowledge in working on business relations to help small business owners who are interested in forming partnerships. You also need knowledge of the tax, state, and federal laws associated with forming business partnerships.
Incorporation	Knowledge of the rules and laws surrounding incorporating a business (forming a corporation).
Business plan development	Knowledge and experience in developing, writing and creating business plans. Business development experience, a business degree, and direct experience in putting business plans together are some of the aspects of succeeding in this area of coaching.

HUMAN INTERACTIONS	
Type of Coaching	**Considerations**
Human Interactions	This niche is concerned with different types of relationships. Having a degree in psychology or sociology, or experience in social work or some other human services field is helpful.

HUMAN INTERACTIONS	
Relationship coach	Having a background in couples' therapy or relationship expertise can be very helpful with this niche. Relationship coaching can be any form of relationship such as parent/child, husband/wife, or co-workers.
Couples coach	The requirements are similar to those of a relationship coach, but this type of coaching narrows down the niche further by work with a couple. Some coaches work with a specific religion as a basis, while others may specialize in nontraditional couples, such as gay or lesbian couples.
Family coach	Expansion of the couples and relationship coaching experience to include the other members of the family, such as children. Generally, this type of coaching is better with face-to-face interactions.
Human interactions coach	This area deals with people that are having difficulties in more than one area of their lives, such as personal relationships, people in the community, and people at work. This coaching helps them develop more meaningful and successful relationships. A background in counseling may be helpful in this area. Or a licensed counselor can offer this specialized coaching service as it may involve going into the community with the person.

HUMAN INTERACTIONS	
Conflict resolution coach	There are many situations in which people can find themselves in a conflict. Sometimes these can escalate to the point that they are involved in a lawsuit. Having a background in mediation or conflict resolution or training in these areas is imperative and is conducted face-to-face.

GENDER AND AGE	
Type of Coaching	**Considerations**
Gender and Age	Both age and gender have their own issues that a coach can address. This may mean that you are a certain age or gender to be more credible. Backgrounds in counseling or degrees in human services with experience may also be beneficial.
Teen coaching	Experience and knowledge working with teenagers who are in conflict with their parents or may be having a difficult time in an aspect of teenage life.
Middle-age coach	Experience going through your middle-age years adds credibility to a coach that helps clients work through middle-age crises and other issues middle-age individuals face in their personal and professional lives.

GENDER AND AGE	
Retirement coach	A background in finance, retirement funds, and estate planning can be useful. Career counseling and transitioning counseling experience can also be helpful to help retired individuals make the transition from employee to retired or to find a post-work career or to open a business.
Women's coach	Experience and knowledge of women's issues such as career and relationships. Women coaches generally do better specializing in coaching women than men.
Men's coach	Experience and knowledge of men's issues such as career and relationships.
Gay and lesbian coach	Experience and knowledge of the issues that gay and lesbian individuals face such as coming out to family and friends, relationships, and dealing with these issues in the workplace.
College-age coach	Going to college is not only about getting an education; it is about discovering who you are and what you want to do with your life. Many times young people go to college with no idea what they want to do, so a coach can help do life planning with the client. A background of working at a university or in career planning may be helpful. A degree in school psychology or education may also be useful.

HEALTH AND FITNESS COACH	
Type of Coaching	**Considerations**
Health and Fitness Coach	These types of coaches are concerned with the well-being of the body, although there can be overlap into other areas of a person's life, such as self esteem and relationships. Being a certified personal trainer or nutritionist is needed in these types of coaching niches.
Personal trainer	These coaches often work with or for a gym and help set up plans for working out, weight loss, or body image. They support the client by meeting with them face-to-face. There are many different places that certify personal trainers that can be found on the Internet. Being in shape and working out on a regular basis is essential for this type of coach.
Nutrition coach	A degree in nutrition, or being a licensed dietitian, can be helpful, and is often necessary, for this type of coaching.
Group fitness coach	These types of coaches usually do workouts with groups of clients and often work at a gym or similar facility. Can offer other personal trainer or nutrition services as well, and can even coach other group fitness coaches on how to teach or train more than one person at a time.

HEALTH AND FITNESS COACH	
Body image coach	Experience working with individuals that face body image challenges such as anorexics and bulimics. Other body image coaches work with those who need help with the fashion and beauty aspect of the body image over the physical body. A coach in this area may want to have a background in fashion and/or fitness.

SPIRITUAL COACH	
Type of Coaching	**Considerations**
Spiritual Coach	This type of coach does not necessarily lead a person on a specific spiritual path, although there are some that do. They help the client find their own path that will bring them enlightenment and spirituality. A background in teaching spirituality may be helpful, or education as a minister or other clergy vocations.
Living spiritual lifestyle	Some people want to incorporate spirituality in all the activities of their lives — relationships, work, and family. A coach in this niche can help direct their client toward these goals. A background in psychology and spirituality is helpful with this niche.

SPIRITUAL COACH	
Law of attraction coach	This is a very popular notion of "like attracts like" that was made famous in the movie and subsequent book The Secret. There are a number of coaches that specialize in helping clients improve their lives through positive thought and actions. A coach would need to be familiar with the concepts and practice of the laws of attraction.
Spiritual journey coach	Some clients want to delve deeper into their spirituality and need assistance making this journey. The journey can be in the form of an actual trip to a sacred shrine in a foreign land or it can be an internal journey. A coach in this area should have specific skills for meditation and guided visualization.

CAREER COACH	
Type of Coaching	**Considerations**
Career Coach	These coaches work with clients for a number of reasons. They can be in a career they want to get out of, they want to start a new career, or they may be getting ready to graduate from college and need to choose a career.

CAREER COACH	
Specific careers (for example, lawyer or doctor) coach	A coach can specialize in a particular career based upon his or her own life experiences and education. These coaches can specialize in the necessary education options, career plans, and even advancement in particular careers. A degree in and experience working in the field is necessary.
College choice coach	These coaches utilize material they gain about the client, such as GPA, career choices, SAT and GRE scores, as well as information about the best schools to apply for and how their clients can improve their chances of acceptance. A background in college admissions is useful.

Franchise coaching

Another option for starting your coaching business is to buy a franchise. The benefit of buying into a coaching franchise is that you essentially buy a "turnkey" business, where all of the plans are built for you and all you have to do is follow the plan to run the business. Franchises have an established business model and provide you with all of the support you need to make the coaching business a successful venture. The problem is that franchise companies have strict sets of rules, which leaves little room for your own creativity. Cost of investing in a franchise can be another drawback because the franchise has set fees and costs involved in buying into one.

For example, if you buy an ActionCOACH (**www.actioncaoch.com**) franchise, you are buying an established business model for running a coaching business. Not only does this franchise offer a business manual you can follow as a guide to run your business, but buying into the franchise also comes with a system that covers sales, marketing, and coaching. You even get your own personal success coach to keep you on track. In addition to your personal success coach, you have access to a global support group and a network of other coaches you share swap ideas with, cheer successes, and share experiences. When you invest money in a franchise, you are investing money in training, materials, and the guidelines you need to follow to run a successful coaching business. Because the business methodology is established, when you open a coaching franchise, you lower your chance of failure as opposed to if you start a coaching business from scratch. Investing in a coaching franchise can help you to avoid making mistakes that can cost a great deal of time and money, which can put your investment at risk for a partial or complete loss.

As is the case with starting any business, buying into a coaching franchise requires an upfront investment. Upfront investment costs may be as small as a few thousand dollars and can go up to hundreds of thousands of dollars — all depending on the franchise. Some franchisors offer financing options so you can finance the purchase and operating expenses of owning and operating the franchise by making monthly payments. When you buy into a franchise, your financial obligations do not end with the purchase. Franchises typically require you to pay an annual fee for using the name, and some even require you to pay a percentage of the profits.

For more information on franchises, the Small Business Administration (SBA) website (**www.sba.gov**) offers a workbook "Is Franchising for Me?" When you go to the SBA website, click on the Business Planner tab to access the guide.

Franchise Gator (**www.franchisegator.com**) also lists franchise opportunities by investment level and industry.

THE HISTORY OF COACHING AND THE ROLE COACHES PLAY

In some way, shape, or form, the business of coaching has been around for hundreds of decades. Though some of the earliest coaches had to forge their own way and find the path to their own successes, these pioneers have since paved the way for the coaches that have come behind them.

The word coach may conjure up many thought or visions. You may also associate the term mostly with sports. An athletic coach knows all the rules of a sport, has experience in the sport, can teach the sport, can strategize during game time, and lead others to victory in a sport. In individual sports, like track and field or gymnastics, coaches take on a more specialized and personal role. This is similar to an executive coach who works one-on-one with a client to help him or her excel in a particular line of work. Just like athletic coaches specialize in certain sports, many executive coaches specialize in certain industries. It really depends on the particular coach's background and experience as to which industry they choose to specialize in.

In the late 1980s, executive coaching made an appearance due to a shifting emphasis on management consulting and leadership training in large corporations. These companies wanted to increase productivity and reduce turnover, and corporations felt this could be accomplished by working with people within the company to determine their goals and the types of jobs they might best be suited for.

During this shift, the duties of human resources expanded as it began to focus on the needs of employees. At the same time, however, downsizing in companies was widespread. Some of the first areas to be cut included managerial education and training to advance employee skills. Businesses just could not continue to provide these programs internally, so higher management sought outside consultants to help train up-and-coming executives, providing them with the skills necessary to be effective managers.

This philosophy translated into greater profits for businesses and less turnover in personnel. People wanted more than just a paycheck at the end of the week; they wanted to have a sense of self-worth, a feeling that their contributions mattered. They wanted to be able to advance up the corporate ladder, which is where the executive coach entered on the scene.

At the time, executive coaches came to fill two important roles in the industry. First, they helped companies arraign profitability and efficiency by hiring the right people to fill the necessary positions. Second, executive coaches helped individuals who were not content in their current job position to find the right job for them. Individuals using executive coaches found themselves a step above their competition because executive coaches taught the individuals the skills they needed to land the high-paying jobs they sought — find the right jobs with the companies they wanted. The executive coaches also provided support and an insider's view into the practice of business management in a manner that added value to the companies and individuals the coaches were working with. Many of the early executive coaches were successful business people themselves, so they had an insider's perspective of what it took to stand out and used this knowledge to teach their clients how to advance in their own careers.

Coaching schools began to develop and offered specialized courses and certifications to meet the demand of professional and well-trained executive coaches. These new schools were providing training in a new frontier, and the results were, at best, hit or miss. In 1992, Thomas Leonard, an experienced financial advisor, created a new coaching school, Coach University. He created a faculty that ranged from business executives and psychologists to actors to teach and prepare its students to be the new executive coaches of tomorrow. The Coach University curriculum was based on the principles of human resources, as well as theories and philosophies from a number of different counseling and psychotherapy methodologies.

Over an eight-week seminar, students at Coach University completed 25 lessons to learn how to become an executive coach. Topics included improving daily habits, personal standards, mannerism of a professional executive, and what it takes to be a better executive coach. After the basics, executive coaches in training moved to two higher levels of curriculum, which exposed the coach to working with a variety of clients and using different strategies to work with and create successful business people, including active listening and management skills.

Coach University offered its classes online and by phone, using webinars or teleclasses to teach students the day's lesson. These formats opened up the accessibility of the course work to a worldwide audience — an audience that had the flexibility of becoming an executive coach so that it fit into their existing lifestyle and schedule.

By the late 1990s, quite a few executive coach training schools formed. Some of the schools even specialized in specific industries. For example, Therapist University and Mentor Coach was established to mentor mental health professionals. In response to the growing popularity of the coaching industry, associations such as the International Coach Federation were created as a professional organization under Coach University to cater to the needs of professionals in the coaching industry.

Executive coaching was about to make another transition, where executive coaching expanded to include a new coaching profession — personal coaching. Personal coach clients consisted of individuals who were looking to enrich the personal side of their lives as opposed to the professional side catered to be executive coaches. With the expansion into personal coaching, coaching schools expanded its curriculum to focus more on setting personal life goals.

Personal coaching helped individuals with personal relationships, spirituality, and finding their purpose in life. Media campaigns and popular talk shows, such as Oprah, started covering topics about "life makeovers," and the services that the newfound personal coaches were providing. The personal coach phenomenon also coincided with the debut of many self-help books written by coaches to help people in their life pursuits.

According to the International Coach Federation (ICF), it is estimated that there are about 30,000 personal coaches in the world.

A personal coach, however, has a much broader base of clients to work with because clients are not limited to a particular industry or profession. Personal coaches work with clients on interpersonal relationships, setting and achieving career goals, breaking bad habits, developing lucrative habits, advancing communication skills, and finding the right mate. Some personal coaches even specialize in niche areas, such as relationships, or even spiritual enlightenment.

The big difference between personal and executive coaching is that the personal coaching clients may not be working on any career or business goals. Executive coaching, on the other hand is usually focused on business management and career advancement — people applying for management positions need skills to be promoted to those levels of management, but may lack those skills. Executive coaches can provide them this knowledge, teaching them how to be highly effective leaders. Companies sometimes hire executive coaches on a freelance basis to teach executives and managers how to manage employees in the most effective way possible. Although hiring executive coaches to fill this role can be expensive for the company, outsourcing the role is less expensive than the company developing and maintaining a management-training program of its own.

Previous Generations of Coaching

In the past, people relied on their peers, families, and even their therapists to help them overcome personal and professional challenges. The problem is that working with family and friends to overcome issues can provide mixed results — sometimes producing a positive outcome, while other times less than optimal results were achieved.

Individuals who turned to professionals for unbiased guidance relied on a therapist. Beyond the fact that using a therapist costs money, the issue that most individuals had with using a therapist is that therapists tend to do sessions once a week in 30- to 60-minute increments. On top of this, therapists often deal with mental-health issues, diagnosing and treating psychological problems rather than personal goal setting. Therefore, a therapist was not always the appropriate solution for working with someone who wants to improve his or her lifestyle, but does not have a diagnosable mental illness.

This is where life coaches hit the scene and filled the gap between amateur advice and professional therapist advice. Personal coaches work with the person in an objective way and allow the client to steer which journey they want to take on their life path. They are not bound by conventional psychotherapy. It is a more personal approach and the coach can modify the ways in which the client alters his or her life path according to personal needs.

An effective personal coach views a client from a big picture point of view, using the person's strengths to help work through his or her weaknesses. A personal coach becomes a mirror to his or her clients to help them see who they truly are and find their way to their life's purpose.

Coaches are professionals who provide a service just as therapists, mentors, soccer coaches, social workers, and many other professionals and volunteers do. Many personal and business coaches work from their homes, but some maintain a professional office — helping clients in local businesses, communities and industries, as well as those outside of their immediate geographic location.

Both types of coaches provide a needed service. Personal coaches are experts in helping people achieve their goals, become better people, and live happier lives. As people reassess their lives, they want to shift their priorities to the things that really matter in life, and coaches help them maneuver through the unchartered waters. Coaches help people grow psychologically, emotionally, and spiritually. They help the client to shift his or her life into alignment, allowing people to find true happiness in their lives, and in addition, encourage them to uplift others around them.

With finding true happiness comes a shift in consciousness. People want more fulfillments out of life. Maslow's Hierarchy of Needs illustrates the basic needs a human has in order to survive. According to Maslow, if a level of this hierarchy is not met, then the person cannot progress to the next level in the hierarchy. Instead, when someone is fixated on the need they are trying to meet, they get stuck in this particular area of the hierarchy and without a way to overcome the obstacle holding them back, they will never make it to the next level.

As times change, people's basic needs are challenged, forcing them to discover new ways to fulfill their needs. Coaches help people shift into new ways of thinking (also referred to as a change of mindset), which helps people adapt to the changes that can offset their balance, providing them

Maslow's Hierarchy of Needs

with the help and support required to meet basic needs and move up in the hierarchy to fulfill higher level needs.

With the invention of and extensive use of the Internet, people are interacting with others around the globe instantly and more often. No longer are people restricted to meeting people who live close to them, nor are they restricted when it comes to sharing ideas and information. They can find friends and people of similar interests all over the world. People even find their significant others and spouses online — fulfilling Maslow's level of love and belongingness.

It is the next three levels of Maslow's Hierarchy — esteem needs, self-actualization, and transcendence — that have become a focus in people's lives. As people choose professions and careers, there are far more options available to help them achieve these needs than there were in previous years. Personal and business coaches are a driving force in allowing people to achieve this level of needs, but many people are looking for deeper meaning in life. Life coaches, or personal coaches, are meeting this demand by helping clients find a purpose in life. Through consultation, they assist their clients in finding ways to drive their lives in a certain direction, according to that purpose.

It is in the areas of self-actualization and transcendence that people find bliss and take complete satisfaction in their lives. The sheer number of people looking for guidance toward this has created an even bigger demand for coaches. Therefore, the job market is exploding to meet this demand and the statistics support this explosion.

A study done by MetrixGlobal in 2005 looked at the benefits of executive coaching in a Fortune 500 company. The results were positive, illustrating that over 70 percent of the respondents indicated that executive coaches had a significant or very significant impact on in the areas of productivity and employee satisfaction.

The Personnel Management association reported a strong correlation between training and coaching, with 86 percent of individuals who have coaching increasing their productivity while only 22 percent increase productivity with training.

According to the Hay Group, an international human resources consultancy agency, 25 to 40 percent of Fortune 500 companies use executive coaches.

In a survey compiled by Manchester, Inc., a career management consulting firm in Jacksonville, Fla., six out of ten organizations offered coaching to their managers and executives, which is a 20 percent increase from the previous year.

THE ROLE OF A COACH

Even when you specialize in a particular area, coaching work has some tasks and roles that are universal. The part that coaches play when interacting with clients is what makes the coach valuable to the clients. Because you are working with the companies as an independent contractor and not an employee, if you do not provide them with the best service then they will turn to another coach to fulfill their needs. As a coach, this means you lose a client, thus losing money and the potential for future and referral business from the client. If you provide poor quality work as an employee, you may get fired and have to find another job, but when you own a business, shoddy work can crumble the entire foundation, putting you out of business fast. Therefore, when reading through what a coach does, think about how you can deliver to keep your own clients satisfied and ready to work with you repeatedly.

To do: Listen to their needs

From the time you are wooing a prospect to the time you sign them as a client, all of your interactions with the individual — be it for their own personal needs or to fulfill a company need — comes down to assessing what the needs of your client are. In fact, this may be the most important part of coaching work because this analysis permits you to determine what services or guidance you can provide to fit the client's needs. Determining and understanding the client's needs allows you to create a proposal to illustrate how your coaching services can help them fulfill their needs.

Listening is one of the primary skills coaches must possess because it allows you to gather as much information about an individual or a company as possible before spewing out potential solutions to the client. Listening and taking in as much information as possible allows you to garner a big picture view of the problem and position your services as a resolution in a confident, educated, and qualified manner.

To do: Gather more details

Even when you think you have all of the information, the odds are good that there is still information you are missing. Your job as a coach is to act as a type of investigator where you are constantly searching for and uncovering more details and more information. As a coach, you must fully understand the situation the client is in before you try to guide them toward the solution.

To do: Analyze the components

Once you have the necessary information, your next task is to analyze all of the information you have gathered. This is the portion of your role where you ask yourself what is causing the problem to occur in the first place. Similar to a doctor considering a patient's symptoms and lifestyle before making a diagnosis, coaching work requires you to uncover the symptoms the client is experiencing before making a diagnosis. By reviewing the symptoms, a coach is able to see how everything links together.

A DAY IN THE LIFE OF A COACH

When you interview for a job, one of the first questions you should ask is, "What does a day in the life of this position look like?" Getting a visual view of what your daily routine will be like as a coach can help you envision whether it is a position you are going to like or one you may end up loathing.

Your days may look slightly different when you first get started because you will have some start-up tasks to get the business off the ground. Once you get the business up and running, you will have more time to focus on obtaining new clients and servicing the clients you already have.

Another thing to take into consideration is that when you first start your coaching business, you will probably be the only employee. When you are the only worker, this means you fill all of the roles that running the business requires — from answering the phone to working with clients on phone sessions. As your business grows and starts to make money, you can start to delegate some of these duties or outsource certain roles so you can focus solely on the moneymaking tasks of the business, which is working with the clients.

Now that all of the disclaimers are out of the way, this is how a coach's daily schedule may look:

A DAY IN THE LIFE OF A COACH	
8 a.m. – 9 a.m.	Check and respond to e-mails and phone/voice mail messages
9 a.m. – 10 a.m.	Conduct online research for current clients
10 a.m. – 11 a.m.	Make phone calls to speak to parties that have information for clients
11 a.m. – noon	Prepare written notes based on your Internet and phone research
Noon – 12:30 p.m.	Lunch
12:30 p.m. – 1 p.m.	Check and respond to e-mails and phone/voicemail messages
1 p.m. – 1:30 p.m.	Prepare for client phone session/ meeting
2 p.m. – 3 p.m.	Phone coaching session with a client
3 p.m. – 3:30 p.m.	Update client file with notes, observations, and recommendations from client phone session
3:30 p.m. – 4 p.m.	Prepare and send follow-up e-mail to client
4 p.m. – 5 p.m.	Marketing tasks: Cold calling, postcard, letter, or e-mail to prospective clients
5 p.m. – 6 p.m.	Prepare to-do list and schedule for tomorrow

Time management

Managing your time wisely is a skill you can learn (if you do not possess it already). As is the case with almost any goal or objective, keeping a written or electronic schedule can help to keep you on track every day. Prepare the next day's schedule the night before, so you can hit the ground running each morning when you arrive at your office — whether you simply walk into your home office or into your rented office space.

The sample schedule breaks the coach's day into 30- and 60-minute segments. You may feel comfortable with these time frames, or you may choose to break your day into shorter or longer segments. Although your daily schedule will look slightly different, there are some tasks that need to be on your schedule every day: responding to e-mails and phone calls, marketing your business, and working with clients. You may receive e-mails all day, but it is important to focus your time reading and responding to e-mails solely during your scheduled time. Reading and responding to e-mails can be a major distraction from focusing on the productive activities you should be focusing on, so before you know it, you have lost hours of time you should have been focusing on making money on e-mails. If you do onsite coaching sessions or go to clients for sessions, rather than completing them by telephone, then there will be days when you are out of the office all day or for extended periods of time. Even on days when you are out of the office, schedule a segment of time to respond to e-mails and phone messages and to perform at least one marketing effort such as sending out a referral request letter to past clients or an e-mail announcement of a new service you are offering.

THE COMMON COACHING PITFALLS

The majority of this book covers how to become the best coach you can, but there are just as many things you do not want to do to be a successful coach. Change is a scary element for most human beings, and the employees and owners of a business you are working with as a coach are no exceptions to this rule. When a coach comes along, assesses the company problems or issues of the individual, and wants to make changes to the way things are done, the delicate balance of the company is shaken, which means you may feel resistance in your advice and implementing your recommendations. The most important thing to remember is that, if done the right way, you can communicate virtually anything you need to urge someone who truly wants change for the better within the organization. On the other hand, if someone resists, there may be nothing you can say to make him or her accept and implement the change.

Arrogance can cost you in more ways than one

Arrogance should be removed from your demeanor and is one of the key things to avoid when working as a coach. You may have the best and most relevant experience and information to move the company or individual toward the goal at hand, but if you come across as arrogant, it may create a lack of belief in you and your methodologies, meaning the client may not hire you. However, do not confuse arrogance with confidence because you should present yourself as someone who knows what you are doing but not to the point where it is all about you instead of being all about the client. As a coach, you want to fully support the individual and the organization, while communicating your recommendations in a diplomatic manner — without stepping on any toes.

Keeping clients in the dark

Open and two-way communication is the key element of any successful relationship. To build successful relationships with your clients, you have to communicate both the good and the bad points with the client. This may include telling the client his or her ideas are wrong or are not working toward helping the company accomplish its goals. If you do not tell your clients everything they need to know from the beginning and throughout the process or if you hide any of the facts, it is more likely that you and your client will fail rather than succeed. *Chapter 11 provides some specific instructions on how to deliver this news to the client in a professional and productive manner.*

There also may be some uncomfortable times when a recommendation you have implemented is not working. Rather than hide this from the client, be proactive and address problems as they arise, always keeping the business owner or managers of the company in the loop. Delivering bad news or admitting that you were not right is only uncomfortable for a moment, but it is far better than keeping up the charade and making the problem worse.

Going overboard

When you work as a coach, it is important to stay on task and focus on the job you were hired to do. This does not in any way mean you should not go above and beyond for your client, but it does mean not to create work that the client does not necessarily need to pad your own pockets. The best way to get repeat work and referral business from an existing client is do the best work you can with the work at hand. If you create a new problem in an effort to garner more work from the client, you are going to have a hard time showing how you add value to the company at the end of the project because the project was not a legitimate problem.

Making promises you cannot keep

Many coaches make the mistake of promising a client they can do something that is impossible to deliver or the coach does not have the ability to do. Most of the time this is done in an effort to please the client, but if the task is not something that is under your scope of knowledge or is simply too much for you to handle, let the client know this. Do not make the assumption that the client wants you to do everything for them. Give your honest recommendations, but realize you are only human and the client is going to respect you a lot more for your honesty.

Many coaches take on jobs they are not experts in with the hope of becoming experts through the learning experience. This may seem like you are being helpful to the client, but rather than help the client, it may simply leave a bad impression of you and your services. This can cause you to lose the client and the revenue you derive from working with them, as well as put future client referrals in jeopardy. If the work the client is requesting or that you are recommending is beyond what you can comfortably complete, do not push yourself into the role. Instead, only make recommendations that you can do without failing or refer the proper person or organization to complete the task at hand. Likewise, it is also important to keep all of the promises you make. If you tell a client you are going to do something, then to uphold your professional reputation and integrity, you better do it.

Paying attention to the wrong people

As you are working on client projects, you may find yourself in contact with and getting on the radar screen of other companies or individuals who need your services. It may be tempting to meet with them and work through their needs as a new prospective client while putting your current client on hold. This may seem like a primary way to create additional work and new business for you and your business, but it may be at the cost of your coaching career.

If you have allotted time to your current client, make sure that you are using the time to focus on his or her needs. Avoid neglecting your current clients with the hope of landing new ones. If you do not provide high quality service to your current clients, chances are good that you may lose the client altogether, which means you are unable to count on the client for their revenue. At the same time, it may frustrate the new client because you do not have enough time to invest in his or her needs. In the end, you end up hurting three individuals or companies: your company and both clients.

Simply schedule a time to meet with the prospective client outside of the time set aside for the current client. Once you sign the new client, you can adjust your daily schedule to dedicate time to each client fairly based on his or her needs. Set deadlines and expectations with the client keeping your total workload in mind. This allows you to provide dedicated and quality service to all of your clients rather than sacrificing one client for another client. *Chapter 8 covers more on refining your time management skills so that you can juggle clients without sacrificing quality for quantity.*

CHECKLIST

✓ Assess whether your personal and financial situation affects what type of coaching you can accomplish.

✓ Decide what types of companies or individuals you can serve and narrow it down by industry and region, if applicable.

✓ Decide which services, products, and advice you want to offer your clients.

✓ See if you can carry out the role of a coach based on the "day-in-the-life" look of a coach.

✓ Recognize and avoid making some of the common mistakes when working with clients.

Chapter 3: Planning a Successful Leap into Coaching

In this chapter, you will:

- Discover the pros and cons of setting up a home office or renting an office space.

- Learn how to set up your home office or rent office space.

- Gather information on office furniture, equipment, and other business essentials you need to get your office ready for work.

- Uncover how to line up professional help and support for your business.

Even if you have coaching experience, setting up your own coaching office can present a challenge. If you have chosen to work as a coach for an established firm, then your office space dilemma is probably decided for you. Otherwise, your first decision when setting up your own coaching company is to decide whether you want to run the business from your home or you need to rent office space. As is the case with almost every decision you make in the business world and in life, there are pros and cons to establishing a home-based office and in setting up an office outside the home.

Coaching is different than being a manicurist or florist. Though manicurists and florists have clients come to their shops to, well, shop, this is not typically the case with coaching work. In fact, if anything, the opposite is true. Most coaches perform their work in their own space and never come in face-to-face contact with their clients. With this in mind, most coaches choose the cost effectiveness and convenience of running their coaching business out of their home rather than renting an office space. Three other choices generally exist for establishing a coaching business space: rent an office space, use a flextime office rental space, or share a space.

Even business coaches that do work with clients on a face-to-face basis typically find it cost effective and beneficial to run the business from a home office. In cases where you are coaching executives, for example, you would most likely travel to the client's business location and conduct training and coaching sessions on-site with the client. Other companies conduct executive management coaching sessions in a retreat environment, which takes you to a resort or hotel location that still does not require you to have an office space to meet with clients.

THE HOME OFFICE

Opening your coaching business as a home-based business may be the most logical choice when it comes to financing your endeavor. After all, if you are already paying rent or paying your mortgage then it does not cost you any additional money to set up your home office. Two key elements you need to keep in mind when deciding if a home office is the right setup for you are:

Determining whether you have the space

Determine whether you have enough privacy in your home to set up an office to conduct business there.

So, take on one issue at a time with the first being the space. If you live alone in a one- or two-bedroom apartment, then you can set up your business in the corner of your dining room or in the guest bedroom. If you live with other people such as your family or have a roommate, then you need to be able to shut out the rest of the world when it is time to talk to a client on the phone or concentrate on your work. Generally, to run a coaching business, you only need an office that is large enough to hold your desk, chair, computer, printer, and phone. Again, most coaches do not meet face-to-face with clients in the coach's office, so it is not usually necessary to have extra space for holding client meetings or welcoming prospective clients into your office.

Coaching will either be your part-time or full-time way of earning income, so it is important to treat your career seriously. If your home office is the home dining room table that you have to clear every night so your family can eat dinner, then the situation is probably not conducive to running your business and serving as your office. Spare bedrooms, a den, garage, the attic, or a finished basement are all viable options for a home office, which allows you a dedicated space you need to work. You can leave your work one night and come back to it the next day and pick up right where you left off.

Children, spouses, and pets may all be wonderful to have in your life, but can also equate to major distractions and interruptions when you are trying to run your coaching business from your home. When you are evaluating whether a home office is right for your coaching business, consider privacy. Does the space you are considering transforming into your office allow for you to work, make phone calls, and talk with clients without the interruption of your domestic life creeping in? For example, setting up your office on the kitchen table or in a corner of your living room where you cannot shut out the rest of the house noise during business hours can end up being more of a hindrance to getting your work done than a private area with a door. There are also some financial benefits to consider when establishing a home office.

The IRS allows you to write off a space in your home that serves as an office full-time. Generally, if your home office takes up 10 percent of the total square footage of your home, then you are able to write off 10 percent of your mortgage (principal and interest) or rent amount, which can offer a significant tax deduction. To write off the amount of your rent or mortgage though, the entire room has to be dedicated to your business.

The Pros
- Saves you from having to pay rent for an office
- Convenient because you do not have to commute
- Saves time and money because you do not have to commute
- Provides a federal tax deduction when you have dedicated space for your office in your home

The Cons
- Blurs the line between your personal and business life
- Is not conducive for times when you do have to have face-to-face meetings
- Requires installation of additional phone lines and uses space in the home for business purposes

HOME OFFICE CHECKLIST

✓ Do you have an enclosed or private area (preferably with a door) where you can shut out the outside world when it is time to work?

✓ Does the home office provide enough space for a desk, computer, printer, and phone?

✓ Do you have the ability to add another phone line to the office?

✓ Is the space heated and air-conditioned?

✓ Do you have storage space for file and supplies?

CASE STUDY: ADVICE FOR NEW COACHES

CJ Hayden
Wings for Business LLC
P.O. Box 225008
San Francisco, CA 94122
(415) 981-8845 phone & fax
(877) 946-4722 toll free in the U.S.
www.getclientsnow.com

CJ Hayden has been coaching professionally since 1992 and specializes in working with small businesses. Because she began coaching so early, there were no training programs or certifications available at the time. She coaches social entrepreneurs, activists, and nonprofit founder/directors — people who are building enterprises to make the world a better place. She began training with The Coaches Training Institute at about the time it was founded, and eventually earned the Certified Professional Co-Active Coach (CPCC) credential.

When Hayden began her business, she did not have many clients to speak of and she had to find a way to acquire some during a time when the Internet was not very widely used. "When I first started, I got most of my clients from networking and speaking in my local area. I have always been very active in associations and nonprofits and continue to be today," she said. As her business matured, her outreach widened to be national and then international. Now, she gets most of my clients from writing books — of which she has three — speaking both live and virtually (via teleclasses and webinars), and Web presence.

When she first started, Hayden had an office. She said it helped her a lot in the early days to have a place to go where her only focus was work. It also gave her more confidence, and more credibility, because her office made her look like a real businessperson. However, that was in the pre-Internet days, and she is not sure she would make the same choices today. "Having the office allowed me to hold ongoing groups and regular workshops at a reasonable cost. But now, I hold more programs by phone and online than I do in person," said Hayden. And because she can attract clients online from all over the world, she does almost all her individual coaching by phone and does not need an office to meet with people.

It is important that when you begin the process of starting your own coaching business, you target your market. "If you are hesitant to choose a target market or specialty because you have too many interests or are not sure where you best fit, then just choose one for now," she said. You can always change your target market later on as you learn more about who you enjoy working with and where you have the most success.

Contrary to popular belief, choosing a market niche does not limit you; it focuses you. Without a focus to your marketing, you will waste time and money, and may see very little in the way of results. "People do not hire coaches to help them with life. They hire coaches to help them with a specific area of life that is of interest to them right now. You have to speak to that interest, or they will hire another coach who does," she said.

FLEXTIME OFFICE SPACE

In most medium and large cities, there are flextime office spaces or shared rental spaces as an option for setting up your coaching business, which can typically be found in the Yellow Pages of your local phone book. Some flextime offices have "flex" in the name, but others use the term "executive" in the listing name. Shared space options allow you to rent a cubicle or office for a monthly fee. In addition to having your own dedicated workspace, these facilities also offer a receptionist to answer your business calls and forward the calls to you wherever you are or to take a message if you are unavailable. Generally, shared space options also provide limited administrative support to help you with tasks such as making copies, sending faxes, and creating correspondence. The flex space also provides you with a business mailing address where clients can send mail and packages and someone at the location to sign for and accept these deliveries.

For all intents and purposes, a flextime office space provides your business with a professional façade. Rather than answering your own phone, a receptionist answers it for you. If for some reason you do have to conduct a face-to-face meeting, you have a professional environment to conduct the meeting. It also provides a place to go to every day to complete your work, which some people need to get motivated and take care of business. Some flextime offices also allow renters to obtain space on an as-needed basis. Rather than pay a monthly fee for a dedicated space, you may have the option to use the facilities when and if you need them. You may opt for the mail and receptionist services to give off a professional appearance to clients and prospective clients calling your office and then book office space or a conference room if and when you need it.

The pros

- Provides a professional front

- Includes office furniture and supplies

- Some administrative support

- Offers a dedicated work space in a professional environment

- Reduces the cost of having to rent an entire office on your own

- Reduces the cost of having to hire staff such as a receptionist or administrative support

The cons

- Costs can range from a couple hundred to $1,000 a month

- There may be limitations on the personal items you can leave behind because the space is shared by other tenants

- The space has office hours so if you are inspired to work at midnight, you probably are not going to be able to access the building

FLEXTIME OFFICE SPACE CHECKLIST

✓ What space is available to you?

✓ What office equipment is included?

✓ Do you have to pay a monthly fee, or can you on an as-needed basis?

✓ Is there a dedicated line for your business? If yes, does your fee payment include someone to answer the line, take messages, and transfer the calls to you?

✓ Do you have storage space for files and supplies?

SHARED OFFICE SPACE

Along similar lines as flex office space, you may also consider sharing office space with another professional such as an accountant or attorney. Many professional service firms rent and occupy office space that is too large for its immediate needs, leaving empty office space unused. At times, these types of professionals are willing to rent out the extra space, which can mean that you obtain an office inside one of these offices or buildings at a reduced rate. Depending on your negotiations with the professional you are renting the space from, you may even be able to share a receptionist and administrative support services.

The pros

- Provides a professional environment at a reduced rate to renting your own office

- Allows you to separate your business and personal life

- Depending on the type of firm you rent from, it may be a referral source of business for you

The cons

- Commute to work

- Using shared items such as the fax machine and the sign on the office has the name of the firm you are renting from rather than your business name

- Creates a rental payment that you would not have with a home office

SHARED OFFICE SPACE CHECKLIST

✓ What space is available to you?

✓ What office equipment is included?

✓ What is the monthly payment?

✓ Is there a dedicated line for your business? If yes, does your fee payment include someone to answer the line, take messages, and transfer the calls to you?

✓ Can you place a business sign outside the office door or on the building?

FORMAL AND PROFESSIONAL OFFICE

The final option for setting up your coaching business is to rent, lease, or buy an office space in an existing building or as a stand-alone building. Options for obtaining a formal office space can range from renting an office condo, floor, or office space in an office building to obtaining a retail space occupied by other stores and professionals such as real estate and insurance agents. This gives you the option to couple your businesses and gain more exposure. For example, if you are opening a marketing-related coaching business, you may want to consider opening an office near other marketing-related businesses such as an advertising agency, graphic designer, or copywriter. Because you all have the same audience, you have a better chance of landing business when a clients comes to meet with the advertising agency and sees your coaching business in the same office complex or retail center. The majority of these options come completely unfurnished and without any type of support staff, so you will have to furnish the office and hire staff as needed. The primary disadvantage to having a formal office is all of the costs involved in establishing and maintaining the office.

Costs

Some of the costs you need to consider before deciding on a formal office space include:

- Upfront costs and down payment for a mortgage, lease, or rental payment (a percentage of the purchase price or first, last and current month's rent payment)

- Insurance costs for keeping the office (liability, fire, theft)

- Installation of phone lines

- Purchase of furniture, equipment, and office decorations

- Alarm system and locks

- Employment of administrative staff

- Housekeeping/cleaning services

- Amenities such as a fridge, coffee maker, and microwave

The pros

- Provides a professional work environment

- Gives your business further exposure

The cons

- Distractions such as package deliveries, the cleaning crew and your administrative staff

- More expensive than any other office option available

FORMAL OFFICE SPACE CHECKLIST

✓ What else does the rental space include (water, utilities)?

✓ What is the monthly payment?

✓ On top of the rental payment, what is it going to cost for electricity, phone service, cleaning, staffing and other expenses?

✓ Will I need to hire staff to help run the office? If yes, how much will this cost for salary and benefits?

✓ Can you place a business sign outside the office door or on the building?

✓ Is the office a short commute from my home?

✓ Is the office conveniently located for business meetings with clients and vendors?

✓ Is the office located near related businesses that may be a referral source for business?

FURNITURE, EQUIPMENT, AND OTHER BUSINESS ESSENTIALS

Whether you decide to establish your coaching business in a home office or rent an office space, you need to determine what furniture, business equipment, and other supplies you need to get your business up and running and operating on a daily basis. These are the minimal necessities you need to get started. As your business continues to grow, your needs may, and probably will, change.

Phone

The primary business tool you need for your coaching business is a telephone. You should have a dedicated phone number for your business, especially if you are working from a home office. The last thing you want is a client calling in the middle of dinner or in the middle of the night and disrupting your personal family time. You may wish to have a telephone with at least two lines or at a very minimum have a one-line phone with call-waiting service. It is very unprofessional for a client to call your office and receive a busy signal, so you want to make sure that even if you are on the phone your clients can still get through to you or to your voice mail. Along the same lines, you also want to have voicemail service connected to your business phone. Voice mail helps to capture calls from clients when you are not in the office, but it also helps you to capture client messages when you are on the other line or do not make it to the phone in time to answer their call.

Because a coach may be out of the office traveling to and from client locations, you also need to have a reliable cell phone or smart phone to conduct business. You may or may not choose to hand out your cell phone number to clients, but a cell phone comes in handy for checking your office voice mail and handling business when and if you are on the road.

Fax

Though you need to have fax capabilities, there are a couple of different ways you can get the fax services you need. First, you can go the traditional route of buying a fax machine and installing a dedicated line in your office for the fax machine. This, of course, requires the cost of purchasing and maintaining the fax machine. An alternative route is to invest in an e-fax service where you can send and receive faxes online through your computer. There are several e-fax services that provide you with a dedicated phone number for your faxes, such as eFax (**www.efax.com**), MyFax (**www.myfax.com**), and RingCentral (**www.ringcentral.com**). Instead of having to install a second phone line in your office, the e-fax service accepts the faxes for you and sends them to your e-mail. Opening your e-faxes is as easy as opening an e-mail and you can read the fax online or print it, if necessary. E-fax services also allow you to send faxes online. If it is a hard-copy document that you need to send, then you will need a scanner to scan the document into your computer. If you are faxing a word processing document or document already on your computer, then you can send it directly from your computer via fax. These services start at $20 a month with pricing depending on the monthly limitation of faxes you can send and receive.

Printer, copier, fax, and scanner

All-in-one printer, copier scanner and fax machines may be a viable option for your office. When you have high volume printing projects, where hundreds of copies need to be made, you can also use an office store such as FedEx Office or Office Depot to help. Your other option is to buy separate machines for your printing, copying, faxing, and scanning needs. The good part of an all-in-one machine is that for a couple hundred dollars or less you will have all of the equipment you need. The downside is if one of the parts breaks then you either have to replace or repair the broken role of the machine or buy a replacement machine.

Computer and computer software

After the telephone, a computer may be the heartbeat of your coaching business. You will need to use your computer for almost all aspects of your business from conducting Internet research to creating client correspondence such as letters, proposals, reports, presentations, and more. If you have to buy a new computer, make sure that you invest in the best computer possible and that it has software capabilities such as word processing, spreadsheets, database management, and some graphic capabilities for creating presentations. If you are planning on being relatively stationary then you can invest in a desktop computer. If your type of coaching work takes you out on the road on a frequent basis then you may want to consider purchasing and using a laptop computer.

You can purchase software such as Microsoft® Office, or you can investigate online (and free) options such as Google Docs (**www.docs.google.com**) where you can create and access documents online. Online offerings such as Google Docs also allow you to share and collaborate on documents with other parties. Even if your business turns you into a road warrior, other programs such as Box (**www.box.net**) allows you to access your documents from any computer. As an added convenience, when you work on a document on one computer, it automatically backs up the update so you always have access to the most recent version of the document you are working on.

Internet access

Most coaches work in one area of the country and have clients spread throughout the United States and even across the globe. This means that Internet access is an essential part of doing business. You will need Internet access for accessing your business e-mail, conducting research, and keeping up with what your competition is doing.

Office furniture

Take inventory of some of the furniture you already own that you can use in your home-based or offsite office. At a very minimum, you need a desk and chair. You may also wish to have a bookshelf or storage area for client files and support materials. Most coaches find a need for a filing cabinet as well, but other coaches have a paperless office, where all of the documents are kept electronically. You can use Dropbox (**www.dropbox. com**), Box (**www.box.net**), and Google Docs to store and access your files electronically no matter what computer you are on.

Business supplies

The other basic business supplies you need may seem like obvious choices but are items that should not be overlooked as you set up your office.

- **Writing instruments**: Make sure you have a supply of your favorite pens and pencils on hand for everything from taking notes while on the phone with a client to signing client contracts. If you use a whiteboard or chalkboard as part of your brainstorming sessions, then you also want to have a supply of colored markers, chalk, and an eraser readily available to you in your office.

- **Paper**: First, standard copier paper is a must for a coaching office. You may wish to buy your paper by the case or at a minimum by the ream. Second, you may want to have some fancier 24-pound paper on hand for creating letters to clients. Depending on your style, you may also want to have spiral-bound notebooks or pads of paper available.

- **Paper fasteners**: A stapler, staples, paper clips (large and small), binder clips, rubber bands, and tape are all essentials to a coaching office. Preparing written reports for clients in duplicate or stapling two-page contracts together are but two of the reasons you need some fastening devices available to you in your office.

- **Envelopes**: Generally, standard size No. 10 mailing envelopes are sufficient for mailing out everything from client invoices to contracts. If you find yourself mailing larger items, you may want to invest in 10- by 13-inch or 9- by 12-inch mailing envelopes. If you plan on running the envelopes through your printer, make sure the envelopes are compatible with your printer.

- **File folders**: If you plan on maintaining your files and records in a filing cabinet, then you need hanging folders and file folders. Hanging and file folders come in various sizes and colors so you can try out different options to find the right ones for you or use a color coding system for your filing needs.

PROFESSIONAL HELP AND SUPPORT

Once you have your office space chosen and stocked with the necessary equipment and supplies, it is time to build a network of professionals to help support and run your business. The extent of the support system you need to build depends on whether you are planning on being the sole employee of a home-based business or if you are establishing an offsite formal office. For example, if you plan on leasing an office space, you may need to hire someone to answer the phone and welcome walk-in traffic (deliveries, mail, maintenance, and cleaning), especially when you are out of the office during normal business hours. Even if you opt for a home-based business office, you will want to build a team of professionals that assist you with certain aspects of your business.

The three primary support role positions you will want to add to your team include a business banker, an accountant, and an attorney. Finding the best one available for your business can be a challenge, but it can also be the bridge that connects the gap between your business and its success. These types of professionals usually have a broad range of experience working with various types of business owners, which can be beneficial to your company because they can provide advice to help you establish and run your business in the most beneficial manner possible. Having these types of professionals on your team can also be a pool of referral business opportunities for your coaching business because they are working with individuals and executives in their own businesses on a regular basis. When you begin your search for professionals such as a lawyer, accountant, and business banker, here are some things to keep in mind:

Experience and qualifications

Try to avoid hiring someone who is a part-time lawyer, accountant, or banker. Focus on hiring professionals that are dedicated to the industry they serve. Make sure they have experience working with other coaches as well as other types of business owners before agreeing to work with them.

Availability

Though you are not asking to be their only client, it is important that the professionals you work with not have so many clients that they cannot fit you into their schedule.

Cost

Cost is not the only factor, but it is a factor when deciding to work with a professional, so expect to pay more for professionals with more skill and experience than their competitors. Intend to shop and compare professionals though until you find the ones with the right experience and the right price for you and your business.

Integrity

To build your coaching business on high moral and ethical standards, you need to hire professionals that work with the same level of integrity.

Compatibility

It may seem trivial, but you also want to like the professionals you hire so that you can work with them on a regular basis as you start your business and as it grows. Make sure you feel confident and comfortable working with the professionals you hire.

Because you may not hire someone with which you have worked with before or know someone who has worked with them before, always ask for references and do your due diligence before hiring anyone by checking those references. Try to obtain references that are similar to your business (home-based or coaches). Ask for and check at least three references from each professional you are considering. Checking references is not an option but rather a requirement to make sure that you are working with the right professional for your business, so when checking references, be sure to ask questions such as what business the reference is in, how long they have been working with the professional, and how the professional has had a positive impact on their business.

Accountant

Though there are some exceptions, the majority of coaches starting and running a business are not accounting experts. Whether or not you are an accounting whiz, hiring an accountant is imperative to starting and maintaining the business financial records. Delegating this important duty to a professional allows you to focus on revenue generating business activities rather than worrying about paying your state sales tax, filing 1099 reports, or generating a profit and loss statement for your business.

One of the primary factors in small businesses failures is maintaining inaccurate and inefficient business and financial records. Having a professional accountant on your team can help to ensure accurate records, and accurate records help to keep your business on the path to success. The role of an accountant in a coaching business typically consists of five main tasks:

- **Small business start-up accounting, sale of a business, or the purchase of a business**: An accountant can establish your business books and record-keeping system so you start out on the right foot. When and if you sell your business, the accountant can help to show the potential buyer and the buyer's accountant how financially sound the business is, where the profits for the business come from, and the assets and liabilities the business has. Finally, if you are purchasing an existing coaching business, the accountant can review the financial records of the business to tell you if the purchase is a wise investment.

- **Creates and implements an accounting system**: A professional accountant can assess the needs of your business to create and implement an accounting system that best fits your business needs.

- **Prepares, reviews, and audits the financial statements of the business:** Professional accountants have the knowhow to accurately prepare your financial records to make sure you are compliant with the IRS and state tax regulations. The accountant can also review and audit the company financial records to offer you advice on changes you need to make in your business and to ensure you are compliant with the laws in case you are ever audited.

- **Tax planning and appeals**: There are many tax laws and loopholes that accountants are knowledgeable about, which they use to help you appropriately plan to minimize your tax obligations. If you run into a tax issue, the accountant also helps you appeal any tax issues that may arise.

- **Prepares income tax returns**: Businesses, depending on the legal structure of the business (sole proprietorship, corporation, LLC) has to file tax forms throughout the year, including the annual federal business tax returns. The accountant prepares and files these forms on your behalf and makes sure you meet the deadlines for each tax form filing.

One of the best ways to find an accountant for your coaching business is to ask family members and friends, especially those who have a small business, who they use for their own tax needs. Interview accountants as you would any professional you are adding to your business support team and make sure you shop around and compare several different accountants before deciding on which one is right for you.

You may be wondering what the difference is between an accountant and a certified public accountant (CPA). A CPA is a professional accountant that has taken and passed a state exam covering business law, accounting, taxes, and auditing. CPAs are also required to have a college degree, although some states allow CPAs to substitute work experience for a college degree.

Is a CPA better than an accountant for your coaching business? It depends on your business needs. Professional accountants can be as sufficient as CPAs when it comes to establishing and maintaining your business books and financial records, so it is better to assess the experience of each accountant or CPA you interview and how his or her experience relates to your business needs.

Lawyer

Even if your business is starting out with one employee (you), a lawyer is an essential member of your business support team. In fact, hiring an attorney is a task you may want to accomplish before you do anything else, including choosing the legal form of your business entity because a lawyer can help guide you to establish your business in the most beneficial manner for your needs. The role of an attorney in your business can be as small or large as you choose it to be. Most people think of an attorney when they need court representation, but there are several additional roles attorneys can play, with some roles keeping you out of court in the first place. Attorney roles include:

- Helping you choose the right business structure
- Creating and reviewing business contracts
- Working on issues that may and do arise with employees
- Assisting with business credit issues including bankruptcy
- Addressing client complaints and issues (major ones)

Banker

With money playing a pivotal role in your coaching business, it is no wonder that hiring a banking institution that fits your needs is imperative. Your business bank handles your checking and savings accounts for your business, but the role of the bank goes beyond these basic business needs. The bank also acts as the tax depository service for your business tax payments and may be a lender to your business if it needs funds to start, grow, or for another need. Generally, you want to establish a relationship with a bank that has a local presence so you have easy access to them when you need them. Financial institutions range from banks and credit unions to credit card, commercial finance, and consumer finance companies.

- **Banking institutions**: Banks, savings and loans, and even commercial banks are traditional financial institutions that most businesses turn to when establishing various types of financial accounts. As a small coaching company, you may wish to turn to the bank where you keep your personal accounts first to see what it offers in the area of business services. Because you already have an established relationship with the institution, it can make it easier and more convenient to handle your business transactions there as well.

- **Credit unions**: Credit unions operate on a similar level to banks; the only difference is the members of the credit union own it. Credit unions tend to offer the same products and services as a traditional bank but at a reduced cost. The issue you may run up against with a credit union is that often it offers personal accounts and services but may not offer the same extent of business products or services, and therefore may not fit your business financial needs.

- **Commercial finance company**: Commercial finance companies deal with the leasing or financing of major equipment. Depending on the type of coach you are, you may or may not have a need for establishing a relationship with this type of finance company. When it comes to leasing, these types of finance companies can provide significant tax advantages, so it is something you need to be aware of in case a need arises.

- **Credit card companies**: In most cases, small business owners are personally responsible for credit card debt and loans for the business. Many coaches use business credit cards and business credit card loans to finance the start-up costs of their business. The disadvantage to using this type of credit is that the interest rates are typically much higher than standard bank, credit union, and other business loans.

- **Consumer finance companies**: Consumer finance companies lend to those who have bad credit, have defaulted on previous loans, or have a hard time obtaining a loan from more traditional lending institutions. Since these types of borrowers are higher risk for the finance company, consumer finance companies tend to charge higher interest rates than other types of lending institutions, and the terms of the loan tend to be shorter and less attractive. Generally, a consumer finance company should be the last stop on your list and only if you cannot obtain credit or loans from one of the other types of institutions.

CHECKLIST

✓ Decide which type of office setup is the most beneficial to your business needs.

✓ Make a list of the furniture, equipment, and supplies you have for your office and the items you need to purchase.

✓ Gather information on and interview members of your support team including attorneys, bookkeepers or accountants, and business bankers.

✓ Choose the right professional for your business in each category.

Chapter 4:
Putting Your Business
Plan in Writing

In this chapter, you will:

- Learn each component that makes up a professional business plan.

- Create a custom business plan for your coaching business that you can use as a guide for running your business and as a tool to obtain business loans and attract investors.

- Get a glimpse of the marketing plan portion of the business plan.

- Discover ways to implement, stick to, and modify your plan.

"If you fail to plan, you plan to fail." As a coach, planning should be in your blood, and this innate sense should relate to planning the launch of your coaching business as well. Though you may be anxious to get your coaching business up and running, creating a written business plan is an essential part of your business before you open. The business plan helps you create a guide that thoroughly describes your coaching business now and where you want to guide the business to in the future. You would not plan a long road trip without first plotting out the most direct route from Point A to Point B. The same holds true for leading a coaching business to success: You need to plot out how you are going to take your business from Point A (where it is now) to Point B (where you want it to be).

BENEFITS OF A BUSINESS PLAN

The benefits of having a written business plan for your business far outweigh the time investment of putting the plan together. One of the primary benefits to writing a business plan for your coaching business is that it provides you with a clear definition of your business ideas and the direction of your business. A business vision is an explanation to keep your business clear in your own mind, to share with current or future employees of your business, and to help you obtain financing for your business. A business plan establishes a solid foundation for you to build on your coaching business and helps you plan how to deal with problems, obstacles, and issues that may arise in your business. A written business plan also lays out a realistic view of what the purpose of the business is and how to overcome potential obstacles in getting the business started and maintaining it by illustrating the time investment required to create a successful coaching business. Another advantage of putting together a business plan is it brings all of the financial data for starting and running the business together because it forces you to analyze the costs to start and maintain the business; perform an analysis of staffing needs now and as you grow, including what types of staff positions you need to fill or outsource; and how you will hire and train the staff for them to make a significant impact on your business.

Although writing a business plan is not a difficult task, there is a lot of thought and research that needs to happen before you write the first word. Gathering this information up-front helps you write a more effective and higher quality business plan. Before you jump right in to creating the business plan for your coaching company, write down the answers to these five questions. Answering these questions will set you in the right direction for writing your plan.

1. Is there a local, regional or industry need for the type of coaching you wish to provide? Is there a niche your business will be able to serve? Does the coaching service you plan to put together fill this need?

2. Is there an adequate market for your coaching business to turn a sufficient profit? Is there too much competition or will it be too expensive to advertise to attract enough customers? Will your customers be able to pay for the services you are offering?

3. Will you be readily available to service your customers? If your coaching business will have a specific location, will it be centrally located to benefit your customers? Is the location affordable?

4. Do you have the skills and resources available to serve your customers? What materials and products do you require to serve your customer needs?

5. What differentiates your coaching business from your competition? What is your USP? What does your business offer a client that is better or different from your competition? Do you have enough qualified employees to provide the service?

You may need to take some time to research the answers to these questions adequately, but knowing the answers places you in a good position to start working on your business plan. Consider the facts you uncover during your research when writing your business plan. Not only does this paint a realistic view of the viability of starting your coaching business, but it also puts the facts and figures into a comprehensive document you can take to a lender to obtain financing for your coach business.

OVERALL COMPONENTS OF A BUSINESS PLAN

A business plan is made up of several different parts. At the end of the business plan, all of these parts work in conjunction with one another to create a written guide you can use to start and run your business.

- **Company description:** One of the first components of the business plan is a complete description of your company and the services it offers to your clients.

- **Marketing plan:** One of the main focus points of the business plan is the marketing plan, which is a component within the business plan. The marketing portion of the business plan is an outline of marketing efforts to advertise your coaching business to attract the customers you are seeking.

- **Business structure:** This portion of the business plan provides a detailed explanation of how you plan to structure and manage your business.

- **Financials:** The final main component of the business plan is a detailed explanation and outline of the expected start-up and operational costs for your coaching business. This portion of the plan describes how you will manage the expenses and costs of your business.

Though this is an overview of the contents of the business plan, there are a lot of subcategories and information that falls into each of these four categories. The rest of this chapter walks you through the outline of a business plan and guides you on what specific and detailed information each portion of the outline should contain.

A business plan is always a work in progress. Though you need a starting point for your business plan to obtain necessary financing and to launch your coaching business, it is typical and advisable to adjust your business plan throughout the first year of business. Because the business plan contains both short- and long-term goals for your business, your goals may change where you need to refocus your short-term efforts. The short-term efforts may also have an effect on your long-term goals.

Update the plan by revising old ideas that did not work with new ideas. Adjustments to the plan should reflect lessons learned from your first few months in business and in an effort to serve your customers better.

Basic outline for a business plan

- Cover page

- Table of contents

- Business description

- Market analysis

- Competitive analysis

- Marketing plan

- Management plan

- Operating procedures

- Personnel

- Business insurance

- Financial data

- Loan applications

- Capital, equipment, and supply list

- Balance sheet

- Break-even analysis

- Pro forma income projections (profit and loss statements)

- Three-year summary

- Detail by month for the first year in business

- Detail by quarters for the second and third years in business

- Assumptions used to make projections

- Pro forma cash flow statements

- Supporting documents

- Tax returns of principals for the last three years

- Personal financial statement

- In the case of a franchised business, a copy of the franchise contract and all supporting documents provided by the franchisor

- Copy of proposed lease or purchase agreement for building space

- Copy of licenses and other legal documents

- Copy of résumés of all principals

- Copies of letters of intent from suppliers and vendors

Cover page

Think of the cover page of your business plan like the cover of a book or your chance to make a good first impression. In essence, the cover page sets the tone and expectations for what the reader can expect the document to contain. A cover should include the title of the business plan and include the name and logo for your business. Also include the date the document is created, your name as the owner of the company, the business address, telephone number, e-mail address, and website.

Table of contents

Following your cover page, include a table of contents to present the contents of the business plan in an organized and logical manner. It shows the reader that you are serious and organized in your thought process for creating and running your coaching business. A table of contents also makes it easy for the reader to find and access information they are looking for in the business plan. A sample table of contents includes:

- Business description

- Market analysis

- Competitive analysis

- Marketing plan

- Management plan

- Financial plan

- Appendices

- Financial statements (list out each statement contained in the plan)

- Supporting documents (list out each document contained in the plan)

- Business description

Many coaches and other types of business owners find it difficult to describe their business when putting together the business plan. This really does not have to be an overwhelming process. In fact, the description of your business may be as little as one paragraph or may stretch as much as one page. The main question you need to answer when describing your business is: What type of coaching business do you plan on having? When answering this question, some of the details you want to include are:

- The legal structure of the business

- The company mission and vision, which describes the purpose for your business to exist

- Specific and measurable goals for the business

- Provide an overview of the business product and service offerings

- Whether the business is new, a franchise, or you are taking over an existing company

- The name of the business and the owner(s)

Market analysis

The market analysis section of the business plan addresses the industry or companies you will be catering to with your coaching services. This area of the business plan probably requires the most amount of research because it requires you to gather data on the coaching specialty or industry you have chosen for your business focus. Trade journals that cater to coaching and trade journals for the industry you plan on serving are all helpful resources for gathering this type of information. The market analysis contains:

- The industry or niche you are targeting

- The current state of the industry or niche (stable, growing, or declining)

- The industry's future that may affect the success of your business

- The demographics of your current and potential customers

- How big your potential market it

- The dollar value of the piece of the market that is potential business for you

Competitive analysis

The next area of the business plan is a review and analysis of your competition. You can learn a lot about the direction of your business based on what your competition is (and is not) doing. You first need to identify who your competitors are, then you need to conduct an in-depth analysis of their business operations. Determine the answers to these questions to help in your analysis:

- What areas, either geographically, industry, or niche, do your competition serve?

- How does your coaching business differ from your competition?

- How does the competition price their products and services and how does this compare to your pricing?

- What experience do your competitors have and how does this compare to your experience?

- Do the competitors have strong name recognition among the target market audience, and how much market share does each competitor have of the market?

- What stage is the competitor in (growing, declining or stable)?

- Why would a customer choose you over your competition? What is your USP?

- What is your competition doing to market its products and services? What is and is not working?

- What are the strengths and weaknesses of your competition and what are your own?

Marketing plan

The marketing plan portion of the business plan provides an in-depth look on all of the advertising and public relations efforts you will use to make potential clients aware of your business. You may offer the best coaching service in the country or the world, but if nobody knows you exist then you are going to have a hard time making sales and making money. *Because the marketing plan plays such a pivotal role in your business plan, Chapter 10 is devoted to developing and implementing a strategic marketing plan to promote your coaching business.* To give you a basic overview of the marketing section of the business plan, this section of the plan contains:

- A description of your target audience(s)

- The menu of products and services along with the pricing

- The types of the marketing and advertising efforts you will use to build your brand, garner the attention of your target market, and convert them into customers

Management plan

The management plan details how you will structure and operate your business. One of the best ways to list these details is by envisioning what running your own coaching business looks like. Do you see yourself working alone handling every facet of the business? Do you want or need to hire employees to handle various tasks, or can you outsource certain tasks to freelancers and third parties without hiring employees?

Though many factors go in creating your management plan, the first thing you need to consider is that you have to be a good manager to make your coaching business successful. Some of the basic characteristics you need to possess (or learn to possess) are commitment, dedication, persistence, and good decision-making skills. When you are running your own coaching business, some decisions have to be made instantly without time to carefully weigh all of the pros and cons. On top of managing yourself, it is also imperative that you can handle the business finances and manage others. Possessing, acquiring, and refining all of these skills require hard work and patience. The management portion of your business plan is ultimately the foundation you are building for the way your business is run.

When you are putting together this portion of the plan, now is the time to be honest with yourself. It is imperative that you analyze whether you have the skills necessary to manage your business. If you are lacking some skills or some need to be polished, this is the time to own up to it and figure out how to make your skills better — take a class, read a book, or work with a business coach.

For the most part, novice coaches may not have experience running a business if they have always been employees. After assessing your own skills, you can quickly see what type of employees you may need to hire to round out and complement your own skills. This should create a well-rounded team that works well together and can handle the extensive responsibilities of running your coaching business.

When writing your management plan, take the time to answer these questions:

- Do you have the background and the experience to run a successful coaching business?

- What are your shortcomings in running a business, and how will you compensate for those shortcomings?

- Which employees, if any, will you need to add to your management team?

- How will your employees' strengths and weaknesses complement your shortcomings?

- What tasks will you assign to each member of the team?

- How will you outline your employees' responsibilities?

- What amount of help do you need to get your business started?

- How will you hire and train employees to be part of your team?

- What salary and benefits will you provide to each team member?

By answering these questions, you can determine how you intend to run your coaching business. Your answers will serve as a guide for you to reach your business goals. Creating this part of the plan can also act as a handbook for employees you may hire in the future.

If you are starting a franchise coaching company, some additional questions you need to answer include:

- Does the management package address your questions and concerns?

- How will the corporate office help you develop your management team?

- What type and amount of assistance does corporate provide on an ongoing basis?

When considering a franchise, be sure to include any specifics from their business plan into your own business plan because many franchises have requirements you need to follow. Some franchise requirements include how many employees you need to hire, which roles the employees need to fill, the training requirements for you as the owner, the training requirements for each employee, and ongoing education and training required. Because a franchise has existing plans in place, including plan details from the plan franchise can also help you start your business off in the right direction.

Financial data

The starting point for your business financial plan is to create a realistic budget for your business. A financial plan includes your start-up and operating costs, so you need to determine how much money you need to open your coaching company for business and how much it is going to cost you to keep the business open week after week, month after month, and year after year.

Start-up budget

When you first start your coaching business, you will have one-time, start-up costs for your business to get it up and running. For example, you may need to purchase equipment to get the business started, but once you buy the equipment, you will not have the expense again until you need to replace it. Keep the answers to these questions in mind when figuring out the start-up costs of your business:

- How much money do you have available?

- How much will it cost to start a franchise (and should be you planning to do so)?

- What other fees or purchases do you have to make to open your doors for business?

- How much money do you need to stay open for business for the next six months to a year?

Here are some examples of start up expenses:

- Computer equipment

- Computer upgrade (or purchase)

- Software

- Scanner

- Copier

- Fax machine

- Office furniture and supplies

- Head set

- Large file cabinet

- New phone

- Stationery

- Desk

- Total initial expenditures

- Licensing

- Utility deposits

- Computer equipment and software

- Office furniture and supplies

- Total capital expenditure (the total amount of all your start up, one-time expenses)

If you are buying into a coaching franchise, you also need to ask yourself:

- Does the corporation have requirements for your operating and start-up costs?

- Does the corporation set your sales and profit goals for you?

- What sales and profit margin are you expected to reach and maintain to hold onto your business franchise?

Each portion of the financial management plan needs a thorough explanation of your projections and how you came to the figures included in the plan. You may need to talk to a financial advisor or an accountant to help you calculate accurate facts and figures. These professionals also provide you with advice, review your research, and formulate reports about your organization to help refine your plan. Be sure to have your preliminary costs, facts, and figures together before seeking the advice of a financial advisor or accountant so they can review the numbers with you and make sure that they are realistic. It also helps the professionals to provide you with the right advice and guidance to achieve your goals.

Operating budget

If you are running your coaching business out of your home office, your operating budget and expenses are probably going to be much lower than if you are renting office space. Take a look at the amount of money you have available to start and run your business, including any furniture and equipment you need to purchase and how much it costs you to keep your phone, lights, and Internet service on. Once you put these figures together, you will have a good handle on the amount of an operating budget required to keep your business afloat.

You should also have a cushion built into your budget in case unexpected expenses arise. The additional cushion of funds can help you keep your financial plan on more sound ground, which can ultimately keep your business from faltering or failing. As you are building your operating budget, revisit the amount of money you have on hand to see if you have enough money to cover the operating business expenses for six months to a year. If not, you may need to take out a loan or find a way to raise the amount you have in savings.

- Your financial plan should include:

- Information on pending loan applications

- The value of your equipment and supplies

- An up-to-date balance sheet

- A break-even analysis

- A detailed profit-and-loss statement (P&L)

The financial portion of your business plan also needs to include an income statement and cash flow projections for the first three years of your business, including back-up documentation and data. You will want to break the statement out on a month-by-month basis, by the quarter, and annually. Compiling these figures can be challenging, but the benefit of building and maintaining a financially sound business far outweighs the time it takes to prepare the statements. Showing that you have a detailed plan for your business also helps you prove to potential lenders and other investors that your business has a solid foundation and is a good investment for them to make a loan on. With the many variables involved in generating the estimates and projected figures for your business, there is not a set formula for coming up with the numbers. One way to get an idea of projected figures is to look at sample coaching company business plans that cover the same industry. One online resource for sample business plans is B Plans (**www.bplans.com**).

Realism is an important factor when you are compiling the financial data for the company. These estimates also do not tend to be carved in stone, so you may need to adjust this information as you open for business and compare actual costs with the estimates you have projected. Be conservative and realistic when compiling your revenue figures. Though high expected income numbers may initially impress potential lenders into investing in your business, if your business is not able to generate a big enough profit, you will have a hard time covering all of your business expenses, including paying back your loan.

CHECKLIST

✓ Write, edit, and consistently update your business plan as your business continues to expand.

Chapter 5:
Setting Your Fees

In this chapter, you will:

- Learn the different ways you can charge clients and how much to charge for your services.

- Uncover how to price your services by doing competitive research of the industry or location.

- How to establish a fee agreement with your clients, how to collect fees, and how to collection the remaining fees.

Before you open your coaching business, you need to determine what services you plan on offering your clients and how you are going to charge for them. For most coaches, setting fees is one of the most difficult tasks in getting started. You may be able to guide an executive toward being a better manager, but when it comes to setting your fees, you may be at a loss on where to start. The good news is that there is not a right and wrong answer to what you should or can charge for your services. You do have to find the balance, though, between what your time is worth and what your clients are willing to pay for the services you provide. Though at first this may sound like an easy task, if you set your prices too low, the end result may be a surplus of low-paying work that takes a lot of your time and barely turns a profit. On the other hand, if you set your costs too high, you may not get enough business to turn a profit.

COMPETITIVE RESEARCH

One of the best places to start with setting your coaching fees is to do some competitive research. Also, take the time to read about each coach's experience and background to see how it compares to your own experience and background. The more experience you have to offer your clients, the higher fee you may be able to warrant for your services. As you start your research, you will also find that different coaches charge differently — by the hour or a flat rate by the service. Though you may not be able find enough coaches that offer the same industry or niche services you plan on offering, you can get an idea of how coaches in general are charging.

Most coaching companies do not list their fee schedules online, while others list at least a range of fees that provide an idea of what they charge. For those that do not list their fees online, you may want to make some phone calls or send an e-mail to speak directly with the coaches. Explain that you are starting a coaching business and are seeking advice on how they price their services. You will find that most coaches are more than willing to share information with you. Find out not only how they charge clients, but their reasons for doing so. For example, a coach may say they charge a flat fee based on the service because clients are leery of getting charged by the hour because they feel they may get taken advantage of. Keep in mind that every coach is different. You can use the information you obtain from your competitive research to form an educated opinion and base your decision on setting your own fees. Later in this chapter, you will learn more about the fee schedules coaches use in order to get a better idea of how you can set your fees.

After you decide how you are going to charge clients and how much you will charge for your services, you also need to:

- **Establish and maintain an accurate fee schedule:** The fees you set must allow you to meet the financial goals of your coaching business. Not only do the fees need to cover your business financial needs, but the fees also need to cover your personal financial needs as well. Add up all of your business and personal expenses to first determine how much money the business needs to bring in to break even. Then you can work backward to determine how many clients you need and what you need to charge.

- **Embrace and believe in your rates:** The first step to being able to sell your clients on the value of your services and to pay the fees you have set is the belief in the value of your experience and service. Once you convince yourself that you are the best person to handle their problem, you will excel in your business and be able to convince clients the value of what you offer is more important than the actual numbers.

- **Accept that you are worthy:** Accept the fact that you are worth the investment clients are making in you. Stop worrying and being afraid about the rates you have set and about communicating the rates to your clients. Your experience, time, and skills are valuable resources to your clients, and it is up to you to show them how and convert prospects into paying clients.

If you are still struggling with setting your rates, you are not alone in the struggle. This is one of the most difficult parts of becoming a coach. Once you set your rates, stick to the fee schedule you have set so you are able to meet your business and personal financial goals. For example, say your goal is to generate $75,000 each year. Here is a breakdown of a financial plan:

Yearly: $75,000

Weekly: $1,442.31 ($75,000 / 52 weeks)

Daily: $288.46 ($1,442.31 / 5 days)

If you charge $50 per hour for your services, this means you have to be able to land six clients for one hour of service per day, or enough client hours to reach almost six hours worth of work each day.

$$\frac{\$288.46}{\$50} = 5.77 \text{ hours}$$

Once you see the figures in writing, it may lead you through multiple revisions to determine a set price. You will need to refine these goals as your business progresses and your experience widens. Other reasons you may change your fees or fee schedule is if you add additional services or products to your menu or reduce the work you provide to clients. Changing your rates is not a daily or even monthly practice, but you should review your pricing once or twice a year, especially as you become more established in your business and industry.

You will also need to think about how this pricing positions you in the marketplace in contrast to your competition. In most markets, you will not be the only coach available to hire, so you will need to price accordingly to what your competition is charging. Look at it from the point of view of a client. When clients are comparing coaches and all of the candidates are equal, the client is likely to select the least expensive service available — it is common sense. If you have the same references and offer the same services as your competition, chances are good that the client will select the coach who can offer the lowest price.

You need to provide a reason for a client to select you over the other coaches available because clients tend to focus on the less-expensive price rather than weighing the pros and cons between coaches. Because a cheaper price can lead to lower quality service, it is important that you can convince the client that your more expensive price comes with a superior level of service. You have to offer something unique, something the client wants but perhaps has not vocalized or considered. If you provide a customized solution to the client, he or she will likely value your service offering over the competition. If you cannot find a differentiation strategy to work with, then you may need to consider adjusting your price level to be more competitive.

It may take time for you to refine the skills required to assess and analyze your competition. You may also run into a problem if you are offering the same services and charging the same fees as your competition. In these circumstances, other coaches can only stay competitive with you (and you with them) if you offer less expensive fees, which mean you are constantly undercutting your price in order to win the client over. Over time, this can have an adverse effect on your business and personal finances. Here are some tips for illustrating the value of your services and fees:

- **Add value:** Figure out a way to differentiate your services from your competition so your services stand out from the rest. For example, charge the client for five objectives, but deliver six. Instead of delivering results in the expected two months, offer delivery in one month or six weeks — but make sure it is a realistic promise you are making. These small things can make a considerable impact on the client's view of you and help you build your reputation.

- **Offer and provide the best customer service available:** Every client wants to feel as if he or she is important to you. Make the client feel like your number one priority by wowing your client with superior customer service. Always do what you say, meet deadlines, keep in touch, and provide clients with a positive attitude starting from when they are prospects and throughout being a client.

- **Stand out from the competition:** Find ways to be unique in what you offer and how you get the job done. Offer 24-hour availability, implement changes based on customer feedback, or do the legwork for your client. Any coach can offer the basic services a client is looking for, but the coach who gets called back to help again is the one who exceeds expectations.

- **Always do your best work:** No matter what, deliver the best service possible every time. If you are helping a client, he or she needs to be your highest priority, and the client should feel that way. This means sticking to your promises, delivering on time, and doing what you say you will do. These small things make a significant impact on the success your client sees in the work you do.

- **Consider the long-term ramifications:** Instead of having to land a steady stream of new clients, a better solution is to rely on your current clients to offer you repeat and referral business. In fact, it costs five times more to get a new client than it does to keep an existing client, according to The Insight Advantage. Focus on providing the highest quality work and resources you can so you get referrals. Position yourself as available and consistent. If you do the work to the client's satisfaction (or exceed client expectations), he or she will continuously come back when they need work, keeping you busy for less money and effort than always trying to land new clients.

CLIENT PERCEPTIONS OF YOUR WORTH

In the businesses world of coaching, you are only worth what a client is willing to pay. When you first start your business, you may not know what the magic number is, and the magic number may vary from client to client. Spending some time working out specific ways to calculate a range of figures helps you feel more comfortable in setting your fees and provides you with some flexibility when talking about your fees with clients. In order to estimate what your clients believe your services are worth, you need to find out what clients believe your service can provide. While the quality of a service may seem high on the list of necessities, some clients value dollar amounts more than they do the quality of a service. The only way you will be able to find out the perceptions your clients have about your service is to talk with them.

First, find out about the specific needs of the client you are talking with. Some clients may know or think they know what their needs are. Ask questions and probe the client until you figure out what their needs are. In many instance, the client has a different view of their needs and your services than you do. Having two different perceptions (your view and their view) can complicate the process, but you can work on molding and changing your clients' perceptions to help show them how your services can resolve their problem. Though you probably will not be able to read your client's mind as to what they are willing to pay for your services, you can assess what their needs are and then put a price tag on the value of the services you can provide to them.

Benefits to hiring coaches:

- Coaches are independent contractors, which mean they work on an as-needed basis, which saves the individual or company money.

- The coach works hand in hand with the client to get the job accomplished.

- If the client is not happy with the quality of the coach's work then they can sever the relationship with the coach and find another coach to work with instead.

- As a third party, you bring an outside and objective view, which is something that the client does not have.

- Business coaches provide clients with a clear picture about the internal and external forces on the company.

- Coaches devote time and attention to fixing the problem or issue the client is facing.

- Clients can pick up the phone and call you when a new need arises.

- It saves a business client money on job position advertising, training, salary, benefits, taxes, and more for hiring an internal coach or training professional for its executives and management.

When you understand the myriad of reasons a coach benefits an individual or company, it helps you position yourself and your services as a benefit to the clients you are pursuing, which helps clients understand your value and worth. Remember, you are a very valuable asset to the clients you serve, so you are worth the investment.

SHOW A COMPANY HOW YOU SAVE IT MONEY

If you are a coach that works with business clients, the bottom line for any company is resolving their problem or issue in the fastest and most cost-effective way possible. Though a client may seem to focus on the price as the bottom line, it is essential for you to focus on the value of your services. Once you establish a solid foundation on how valuable your services can be to them, then you talk fees and figures for getting the job done.

For example: You start your meeting with a client by stating you charge $100 per hour. The client may get so hung up on the cost that they close their mind off to the rest of your conversation. Now, you have to back pedal to try to get the client to understand the value of what they are getting for the $100 per hour. If the company is paying their employees $25 an hour, you are going to have a hard time convincing them that you are saving them money when they will be paying you $100 an hour. Instead, walk into the meeting and discuss the client's need first. This allows you to gather information, such as the fact that they pay their employees $25 per hour. You can then explain how hiring an employee to complete the coaching or training role you would fulfill is going to take the employee 40 hours per week to complete at $25 an hour. Hiring you as a coach, on the other hand, means the task is complete in one month for a total of 40 hours at $100 per hour, which is a significant cost savings for the client even though your hourly fee is four times as much.

To help clients understand your worth, you can break it down into figures. Money tends to talk and be the determining factor, so showing a client how you save them money can be a compelling exercise in gaining their business. So, the hourly rate pay for the employee is $25 an hour, but that comes with the 35 percent (on average) the company has to pay for the fringe benefits such as health and life insurance and retirement plans. An employee also comes with the added overhead (50 percent on average) paying for expenses such as workspace and electricity. With these additional costs, the client ends up paying about $46 an hour for an employee to tackle the issue you would be tackling as a freelance coach.

Benefit cost per hour: $25 x .35 = $8.75

Overhead cost per hour: $25 x .50 = $12.50

Total cost per hour: $8.75 + $12.50 = $46.25

That employee is going to stay on the payroll even when the issue is resolved, while you get the job done in a total of 40 hours and in a one-month period. In effect, hiring an employee would cost the company more than $96,000 a year.

Weekly cost: $46.25 x 40 hours/week = $1,850

Yearly cost: $1,850 x 52 weeks = $96,200

Instead, if the company hires you to work 40 hours a month for $100 an hour, the company is paying $48,000 a year. This is more than a 50 percent savings to the client.

Monthly wage: $100 x 40 hours = $4,000

Yearly cost: $4,000 x 12 months = $48,000

FEE OPTIONS

With two basic ways you can charge clients for your coaching services, it is important to understand how each option works. Then you need to understand the pros and cons of each fee structure. Finally, it is vital to understand in which situations each fee structure may be most appropriate for the client and most beneficial to you and your business.

Hourly

One of the primary ways coaches charge for their services is at an hourly rate. As is the case with any fee method, there are pros and cons to using an hourly rate to charge your coaching clients. The biggest disadvantage is that clients may feel like you are taking longer than necessary to help them work through their issue or reach their goal in order to inflate your fees. You may also find yourself consciously or unconsciously working more hours with the client in order to make enough money to cover your expenses. Either way, this type of fee schedule tends to pit the coach and the client against each other and can cause a variety of rifts.

However, you will find other clients who prefer to work on an hourly basis. This is especially the case when you correctly price your hourly rate. If you price your hourly rate too low, you may have to work twice as many hours to make enough money to live on. If you price your hourly rate too high, you may not be able to attract enough business to make enough money to live either. When you are conducting your competitive research and talking with other coaches, gather the hourly rates for the coaches who charge by the hour. Most likely, the figures you obtain from other coaches run a wide range. This range provides you with a sliding scale that you can use to determine your own rates.

You also can use two other methods to calculate a range of hourly rate possibilities. One way is to build your hourly rate from the bottom up. For example, if you were working as an employee for a company, you would probably have a set number of hours to work for each pay period. If you divide the salary by the number of hours, you can quickly determine the hourly rate you are making as an employee. So, assume your weekly (gross) salary is $1,500 and you work 40 hours per week.

Hourly rate: $1,500 / 40 = $37.50

This calculation provides you with a base rate of pay you need to charge your coaching clients to make a comparable income that you would make as a company employee. On top of this base rate, you need to add the cost of your health insurance, retirement plan, and other expenses. Therefore, instead of needing to charge $37.50 per hour, you may need to charge an hourly fee closer to $50 an hour to pay yourself as a coach and cover your own business expenses.

Another approach to calculating your hourly fee is to build the rate per hour from the top down. If you know you need to gross a certain amount of money each month, then use this as a base figure and work your way down from this figure. So, if you know you need to bring in $10,000 per month, use this figure to determine how many hours of work you need to make this happen. Then, divide the number of hours of work per month into the amount of money you want to make to determine your hourly rate.

Hourly rate: $10,000 / 160 = $62.50

No matter which method you use, the market must have the ability to support that dollar amount to make your business profitable. If you are able to convince the client that you are the right person for the job based on your value, then the client is less likely to be concerned about what your rate is (within reason, of course). Most businesses and clients assume a 20 to 30 percent markup on the standard going rate for a coach to receive a superior level of service. If the client believes you can provide the quality of service they are looking for, then they do not tend to mind paying premium pricing for it.

Retainer fee structure

Retainers are popular fee structure with professionals such as attorneys, accountants, and coaches. A retainer is a type of flat-rate fee structure where a client pays a monthly set rate and has relatively unlimited access to you and your services. The retainer fee is typically set based on a projection of the clients' needs so the client is not overpaying and the coach is not overworked and underpaid.

For example, a marketing coach may charge a client a retainer fee of $2,000 per month. The client can use the coach's marketing services as often as they like for the $2,000 per month. Even if the client does not contact or use the marketing services for month, the coach still receives the $2,000 fee. On the other hand, if the client calls the coach every weekday for the entire month, the coach also receives the $2,000 retainer fee.

One of the main benefits of a retainer fee structure is it allows coaches to earn money that is not directly linked to meeting a set goal or working a set amount of hours. Clients can also benefit from this fee structure because they know they can call you at any time about any of their needs because they have retained your services without limitation.

Some coaches allow clients who do not use up the retainer fee for one month to roll it over to the next month. For example, if your client contracts you with a retainer for $10,000 of services a month, you assign a time limit for this amount of services (in your client's file, but not necessarily to the client). If in January your client only uses $5,000 worth of the retainer, then the additional $5,000 balance of the retainer fee is rolled over to February. If in March the client uses $12,000 worth of your services, then he or she may be required to pay you an additional $2,000 because it exceeded the $10,000 retainer fee. Some coaches allow clients to deduct this overage amount from the next month's retainer. At the end of the year, all balances return to zero and the client starts all over again, so balances are carried from year to year. The bottom line with a retainer fee is that you still have to determine how many hours you "owe" the client for it to be fair for both you and the client. If you expect to earn $100 per hour and your retainer fee is $5,000 per month, then is essence you intend to allocate 50 hours per month to the client.

Setting your fees on a retainer basis can be beneficial because it establishes a long-term relationship with your client at a set dollar amount. It is consistent work, which is vital to operating a financially successful coaching business. Though retainer fee structures have several benefits, there are also drawbacks to this type of relationship. You can allocate a certain amount of time each month to work on your clients' work and then take on additional clients to fill up some of your "free" time, but what if a retainer client is additionally needy one month? You may have difficulty getting all of your work accomplished.

ONCE THE PRICE IS RIGHT

Once you set your rate and choose the method of charging clients, you can start working toward attracting clients. Before you pull out your megaphone and announce your business is open and accepting new clientele, it is time to establish a fee agreement and plan on your process for collecting payments from clients.

A fee agreement is a written instrument used to spell out your agreement with the client. Determine how to space out payments for your clients and include it in the agreement or contract. For example, if you work with a client and provide them with an hourly fee and an estimated number of hours to reach the goal of your coaching sessions, you may collect a 50 percent deposit up-front and the remaining 50 percent when the project is complete. Other coaches invoice the client on a set schedule, such as monthly, for the number of hours they worked with the client in the month.

The key to successful payment agreements and collection is to be as detailed as possible when putting together the written agreement. Make sure your agreement spells out who you are, who the client is, the scope of the work you will be doing together, and the specific payment terms. Require a signature from the client, and make sure that you maintain an original copy of the signed agreement in case conflicts arise in the future.

You should require a deposit from all clients before you start to work with them. This protects you from working for free for a client that does not end up paying your invoice. Collecting a deposit up-front means the client has a stake in the relationship and reduces your chances of working for nothing. Even clients that hire you on a retainer should be required to give a deposit up front. Again, the amount of this deposit is something that has to make you and the client feel comfortable. Some coaches require their clients to pay the entire retainer amount up-front, which is why they allow clients to rollover unused amounts to the following month.

IF YOUR RATE NO LONGER FITS

No matter what type of fee structure you decide on, there may be circumstances where you need to change the rate you are charging a client. A rate change may occur on an individual basis or there may be circumstances where you have to change your overall rates across the board. Prices may warrant a change because the cost of living increases, you have more experience, or because a client is requiring more from you than you originally agreed upon.

As a coach, you may find it hard to increase your rate. You may fear that a rate change will cause you to lose the clients you already have or scare away the prospects you are trying to win over. On the other hand, you may need to reduce your rates for circumstances such as a change in the market for your services where you will not be able to obtain a client at your current rate. The key thing to remember is that making changes to your rates requires a careful thought process and adequate planning.

A fee agreement will include special circumstances or stipulations where rates may change if certain circumstances occur. This is something you want to anticipate before it happens rather than after.

When to increase

The primary reason for increasing your coaching fee is that some circumstance has arisen where it is going to eat away at your profit. There are some reasons that only apply to a specific type of coaching business, but most factors apply to any type of coaching business.

Most coaches who see a need to increase their rate charge it to new clients rather than increase the rate for existing clients. In essence, a new client does not see the rate increase because you are simply starting them out at the higher rate. For clients you are currently under contract with, you may need to wait until your contract is up for renewal before you can incorporate your new rates and fees. However, if there are charges unaccounted for in the contract or agreement, you will need to discuss these circumstances with your clients. In some cases, the client is willing to work with you to cover these additional costs. Other clients may walk away from your relationship because of the additional fees. Here are some reasons when you should consider raising your rates:

- **Testing the marketplace**: During the first few months of your coaching career, you will probably be testing the marketplace to see if clients are willing to pay your fee, and whether your fee is adequate for the time and effort you are putting in. Setting your fees accurately means determining the right fee based on what the market is willing to pay for the services you provide. If you increase your rates, evaluate how this changes the number of clients and amount of work you have. If the increase in rate causes you to lose the majority of your clients and you no longer have enough work to sustain your career and business, then you may have to reconsider.

- **You underpriced your services**: If your profit is suffering or you are not profiting at all, then you may have to change your rate. In this circumstance, increasing your rate is a matter of necessity because your coaching business may fail completely if you are not making enough money to exceed the amount of your expenses.

- **Additional expenses:** Often you do not realize the costs involved with working with a client until the relationship begins. For example, you may need to have a membership in their association to provide service to them. Perhaps there are travel expenses you might not have known about ahead of time occur or the work with the client is taking more time than your time allocation. Each of these circumstances can hinder the value of your business if you do not increase your rates.

Although these are some of the reasons to increase your rates, other factors may require rate increases. The key is to remember that you should only raise your rates when you have a reason to do so.

Decreasing your rate

Reducing your coaching rates should only occur if you can still turn a profit and is in the best interest of your company. Decreased rates may be necessary, but never lower your rates unless you have a solid reason for doing so. Ultimately, you still need to make a profit to keep your business open and to earn enough income to live. Before you consider a decrease in your rate, carefully consider how the changes may affect your ability to cover your expenses and unexpected fees associated with your business. Here are some reasons why you may need to reduce the rate that you charge to your clients:

- **Your services are overpriced**: When you first open your coaching business, a common situation is to overprice your services for your local market. If you price your services too high for the market, then you will not attract enough clients to make your business profitable. After you have exhausted all of the possibilities of attracting clients, such as adjusting your advertising, networking with new people, and reducing your expenses, the next step is to adjust your prices down to the market level.

- **You want to reward your long-term clients**: Sometimes it is good business to offer a discount to your long-term clients. For example, if a client refers a lot of business to you, you can reward him or her by offering a discount on your services. When you want to do something like this, it is often best to make it a one-time thing rather than a standard rate decrease. For example, you may offer a discount on your services for one month of the client's contract rather than for the entire term of the agreement. This way, you still are turning a nice profit, while showing your appreciation at the same time.

- You want to network with other professionals: In some situations, you should consider offering a discount on your services, when feasible, to those you are working with in your coaching business. For example, you may want to offer a discount to a company that works with your target market. When the other professional has a client that requires your services, they tend to call on you first.

- **You want to get your business off the ground**: There is no doubt that all beginning coaches struggle to get their first few clients under their belt, so they may price their services lower to attract the first few clients. But, during this time, you are also likely to spend money on advertising and setting up your business. For this reason, be careful about setting your costs too low, or you may be shutting the business down before it gets off the ground. Once you have started to acquire business, gradually work to build your profit margin back up because experience is a helpful tool in justifying higher rates.

Some coaches offer new clients an introductory rate on their services, which is a step that can help you establish long-term contracts with clients. However, you still need to communicate your reduced introductory rate while making sure that they know what your regular rate is to illustrate the value the client is receiving for the reduced rate. For example, in the fee agreement list your normal pricing model along with the introductory rate. Point out the savings the client is receiving by working with you and advise them it is a one-time discount for the initial service offering.

When clients want a reduced rate

You will most likely run into clients that want a reduced rate no matter how low your rates already are. Price shoppers will approach you with a quote from your competitor that is lower than your own price quote. If you have done your research up-front, you know the fair price for your services, but even more, you know the importance of turning a profit in your business. When a client wants a reduced rate and you cannot justify it, take a stand and let them know that you are not able to provide your services at a lower rate. Keep in mind that you are responsible for setting your rates, not the client.

If you do not want to lower your rates, then say no. Explain to prospective clients that your rates are based on research, expenses, and skill, and therefore the value you add to the client warrants the higher rate. Be prepared to have and share all of the reasons why your service requires the higher rate. For example, you could say: "My rates are based on 30 years of experience in the field. Your other quote is for someone just starting out in this business." This puts it back on the client to decide if quality is worth the difference in cost to them.

In other situations, it is necessary and helpful for you to consider a counter-proposal. If they are asking for a 10 percent reduction in your fees, consider offering them a 5 percent reduction instead, as long as you still turn enough of a profit for your business. Rate reductions can be beneficial for coaches starting out. Ultimately, it is all about creating a financially successful coaching business, and if you continue to undercut your rate at the expense of the business then it is not worth it.

CHECKLIST

✓ Decide how you will charge clients for your coaching services.

✓ Conduct research on competitors to find out what they offer and their fee structure.

✓ Set your prices and fees for each service you will provide.

✓ Create a written template of your client fee agreement to use as the basis for creating a contract between you and the client and collect fees due to you.

Chapter 6:
The Legalities of
Starting Your Business

In this chapter, you will:

- Learn several of the legal aspects to consider when opening a coaching business.

- Become familiar with the different business structures.

- Learn the different tax structures for each type of business entity.

- Uncover how to choose and register a business name, including trademarks.

- See how to obtain a business or occupational license.

- Deal with obtaining necessary permits for your business.

- Learn how and when to obtain an employer identification number (EIN).

- Discover how to deal with state sales tax.

Starting your business off by establishing a legal entity is the first step in the life of your business. It can save you headaches, fines, and additional fees in the future as well as helping your business to be more successful and more profitable. Although the right knowledge, skills, and equipment are all necessary to run a successful business, you also need to have the right legal setup for your business. Several different factors need to be considered when determining which type of business entity is the most beneficial for your coaching business. Each legal business structure has benefits and drawbacks associated with it. When you are putting your business plan together, talk with your attorney and accountant to answer any questions you may have about establishing the legal structure of your coaching business.

Before you choose a business structure, first you want to come up with a name for your coaching business. The following is a list of eight common mistakes people make when choosing a name for their coaching business:

MISTAKE NO. 1: YOUR NAME DOES NOT STAND OUT ENOUGH

It should reflect your niche and uniqueness. Suppose you are a spiritual coach and name your business Jane's Coaching, which is rather plain and common and may not attract attention. To make the coaching business name stand out, you may consider the name "Spirit Reclaimed" instead. It describes the service you provide in more of a creative manner.

MISTAKE NO. 2: STICKING WORDS TOGETHER

A common approach for coaches trying to come up with a good name for their business is to stick words or parts of words together. Most often this is in the form of sticking an adjective in front of a noun. Here are some made up examples:

- Tranquicoach

- Intellicoach

- Dynacoach

- Superlife

You want a name that attracts the right kind of audience, and smashing words together can sound a little forced. Take your time and come up with a catchy name that feels easy to read and say.

MISTAKE NO. 3: USING SCRABBLE® TILES TO CREATE A NAME

Some coaches believe that using different letters to spell a word is creative. A common replacement is using a "ph" for an "f," or a "k" instead of a "q." Here are some examples:

- Phinelife

- Uneeke Coaching

- Kwalitcoach

Though it may make it easier to obtain a domain name for your business' website, it could make it hard for potential clients to find you. You may end up buying other website domain names that would cover misspellings of your business name. Here is an example:

- www.phinelife.com

- www.finelife.com

- www.phineliphe.com

- www.fineliphe.com

There are company names that are made up words that have become very successful — Xerox, Google, or Kodak. These made-up words have no linguistic or intrinsic meaning; they are new words that have a lot of advertising and strong brand identification behind each. This kind of branding can cost millions of dollars to create, so unless you have a large budget to begin with, you may want to shy away from creating a new word as your business name.

MISTAKE NO. 4: HAVING TOO MANY OPINIONS

Friends, family, and colleagues can all have the best of intentions when helping you come up with a great name for your coaching business. In the end, you have to make the final decision in choosing the name for your coaching business. Find a couple of pragmatic, right-brained people; involving left-brained people may come up with a name that is too overly descriptive and too literal.

MISTAKE NO. 5: PUTTING YOUR COMPANY ON THE MAP

Some coaches feel their location is important for their business, and this may be true. However, if you intend to do most of your work online or by phone, your location may be irrelevant. It is important to consider this before adding a geographic locator to your coaching business name.

If you are targeting a particular market that involves a geographic location, then using a name like California Coaching Inc., might work. That way if a person places coaching and California as keywords in a search engine, your business will more than likely come up. Just be aware that your coaching business may grow beyond your geographic area, so using a place name in your business name can be limiting.

> Many people know the company 3M. Did you know that original-ly is was called Minnesota Manufacturing and Mining? Because they expanded well beyond the borders of Minnesota, they had to change their name.

MISTAKE NO. 6: TRYING TO MAKE YOUR NAME MEAN SOMETHING

Sometimes a name will seem like a good business name because it holds meaning and significance for you. But what does it mean to everyone else? Will potential clients have any idea of the story behind the name? Does the name truly reflect your coaching business and niche?

This is not to say that having a business name with a story behind it is necessarily bad. In fact, it can be a powerful branding technique that can tell the story of business. If you choose something that is too hard to say, spell, or remember, then it may not be a good idea to choose it as your company's name.

Suppose you want to name your coaching business "Blue Orchid." This may seem odd to many people, but it can be intriguing. If you have a good story or explanation to go along with it, then it can be a powerful image. Suppose a blue orchid means that everyone has beauty within that needs to be cultivated and coached along. Maybe you once grew a blue orchid and because someone saw what a great gardener you were, they gave you a job, which turned into a 20-year career in the landscaping business.

MISTAKE NO. 7: USING CLICHÉS AND METAPHORS

Some coaches find that they cannot think of a good name and begin working with metaphors. These types of business names are not inherently bad, but some words can be overused and therefore can appear cliché and very commonplace. Consider the overworked words: Peak, Top, Apex, Pinnacle, and many other similar words. Work at it and look at other coaching business names online. You may see patterns of words that you want to avoid.

MISTAKE NO. 8: BEING STUBBORN

Nobody is perfect, and mistakes can easily be made when choosing a business name. What makes it worse is pretending it is a great name and that people just need to get used to it. That mindset will cost you money. For example, PODS (Portable on Demand Storage) company was originally called Portables, which made many people think that the company dealt in portable bathrooms (port-potties) or portable classrooms. Once they changed the name, the company exploded with business because the new company name better reflected what the company offers.

Once you have chosen a name for your business, then it is time to choose a structure for your business.

SOLE PROPRIETORSHIP

When starting a business, this is perhaps the simplest and least expensive way to establish the legal structure of your business. To establish a sole proprietorship, all you have to do is choose a business location (be it your home or a rented space), acquire any necessary equipment, and open your door for business. The attorney fees for setting up a sole proprietorship are far less than establishing any other type of business entity and you can typically set up a sole proprietorship without hiring an attorney at all. Even better, as the coach and the business owner of the coaching business, you have complete authority over all aspects of the business. Sole proprietors can operate any type of business on a full-time or part-time basis. Some sole proprietorship businesses include:

- Store or retail business

- Unincorporated company with one owner

- Home-based businesses

- Coaching firm with only one coach

One of the major drawbacks of establishing your coaching business as a sole proprietorship is that you are personally liable for the business in all regards. If a client sues you for a business act, they can go after your personal assets. The business operator of a sole proprietorship is also personally liable for any loans or expenses of the company.

Sole proprietors are required to maintain company records that are in compliance with federal tax requirements for business records. This means they must file federal taxes using the Schedule C or C-EZ (Form 1040), Net Profit from Business, when they file their personal tax returns. The net business income or loss for a sole proprietor is included with any other revenue you receive and deductions you make. A sole proprietor is taxed at the individual tax rate on the personal tax return. Sole proprietors may choose to pay self-employment tax on the net income they claim using Schedule C. Sole proprietors may also be eligible to deduct half of the self-employment tax on Form 1040 using Schedule SE (Form 1040), Self-employment Tax, to calculate the amount of the tax. Sole proprietors do not have taxes withheld from their business income, so in order to make a profit it is typical for the sole proprietor to make quarterly tax payments, which are estimates based on the expected business income for the year and include income tax and self-employment taxes for social security and Medicare.

PARTNERSHIP

A partnership forms when you share the ownership of your coaching business with at least one other person. The two most common forms of business partnerships are general partnerships and limited partnerships. Though establishing a general partnership only requires an oral agreement, legal paperwork should be drawn up to make sure business items remain in order. The goal of a written agreement is to safeguard the business against problems and disputes that may arise between the partners of the coaching business. In a partnership, you and your partner are equally responsible for your own actions regarding business conduct and liabilities. There are some legal fees involved in creating the partnership agreement, although these costs are minimal and typically worth the investment.

A partnership is not required to pay income tax, but each individual partner is required to file Form 1065, U.S. Return of Partnership Income, to report the revenue and expenses for the partner. Form 1065 is an information form used to pass the information through to be included on the Schedule K-1, Partner's Share of Income, Credits, and Deductions, of the individual partners. Each partner then reports the net profit or loss of their portion of the partnership on personal tax returns (Form 1040). Similar to sole proprietors, partners usually make quarterly tax payments, which are estimates of the expected portion of the profit.

If you are the general partner in a partnership, then you are required by the IRS to pay a self-employment tax, which is calculated from your net income from the partnership. If you are a limited partner, you are required by the IRS to pay self-employment tax on the amount of income you receive for any services that you personally rendered to clients.

CORPORATION

A corporation is a business entity that stands on its own. Most coaching businesses do not start out as a corporation and most never become one. When a coaching firm becomes a corporation, the businesses control is in the hands of the stockholders of the corporation. You do not need an attorney to incorporate your business but having legal advice to do so can help you avoid problems or difficult situations. Corporations cost more to organize and are much more complicated to set up than other forms of business, but it is possible to create a corporation that is less formal than larger corporations are. Corporate entities are required to keep organized and detailed written records, some of which have to be filed with the state where the corporation has its corporate headquarters. In terms of liability, the officers of the corporation are legally liable to the stockholders for any improper behavior or situations that may arise within business operations. This means that if the officers of a corporation do something that causes the business profits to go, which in turn affects the return on investment to stockholders in the company, then the officers are going to have to explain what caused the change and how they plan to correct the issue.

Shareholders of a corporation are responsible for paying tax on any dividends received from the corporation, which is reported on the shareholders' personal tax returns. The corporation is treated as an entity, so the corporation is responsible for paying taxes at the corporate tax rate. Corporations file tax Forms 1120 or 1120-A, U.S. Corporation Income Tax Return. If an employee of a corporation is also a shareholder of the corporation, then the employee is responsible for paying income tax earned as an employee for the company. The employee pays 50 percent of the social security and Medicare taxes charged on the amount of their income and the corporation is responsible for paying the other 50 percent.

S CORPORATION

A subchapter S Corporation is a type of corporation that permits the income or loss of the business to be passed through to individual tax returns of the business owners. Other than the way business income and loss is treated, a subchapter S Corporation operates the same way a corporation does. Generally, an S Corporation is treated similar to a partnership so it is not required to pay federal income tax, except specific capital gains and passive income. Rather than filing Form 1120 like general corporations, S Corporations file Form 1120-S, U.S. Corporation Income Tax Return for an S Corporation. Each shareholder must complete Schedule K-1, Shareholder's Share of Income, Credits, and Deductions, which is included with Form 1120-S for each shareholder. The income is also reported on the shareholders' individual tax returns.

LIMITED LIABILITY COMPANY (LLC)

Another type of business setup is a limited liability company (LLC). An LLC possesses many of the same benefits that a corporation does. As a coach, you will find that an LLC may be the most beneficial form of business because it limits your personal liability for company liabilities and legal issues. An LLC also offers you tax benefits that differ from a sole proprietorship or partnership coaching business, but an LLC does allow pass-through taxation.

Owners of an LLC are called members, which can be individuals, corporations, other LLCs and foreign entities. In some instances, an LLC only contains one member (one owner). Publication 3402, Tax Issues for Limited Liability Companies, available on the IRS website (**www.irs.gov**) provides specific information on the tax return forms LLCs must and how to handle employment taxes. In short, an LLC offers you more flexibility in your business setup and provides you with more options in how you can manage and operate your coaching business.

GOVERNMENTAL REQUIREMENTS

Each state, county, and city in the United States has its own laws you must adhere to as well. You need to become familiar with the various requirements to establish your business legally and avoid future fines and problems from arising. This laws and regulations include everything from the zoning requirements where you can run your business and scheduling and passing required inspections to having the appropriate licenses and permits to run your business. The U.S. Business Advisor's website at **www. business.gov** provides helpful information to those looking to start a business, which includes:

- A business resource library

- Online counseling services

- Information on financial resources available to start-up businesses

- Links to laws affecting different industries

- Legal and regulatory information for small businesses of all kinds

- Plenty of other helpful tools are available to locate reliable information on starting a business.

The Small Business Administration (**www.sba.gov/advo/laws**) includes a list of coaches that service various industries and that provide a variety of services.

The IRS (**www.irs.gov**) helps prepare your business tax information and forms

The U.S. Department of Labor (**www.dol.gov**) can help you manage employees and learn minimum requirements for working environments and other employment law and regulation information

Each state offers other resources from the state's department of business, which may also be called the state's Department of Development office.

One example of these helpful government-sponsored websites is Ohio's 1st Stop Business Connection (**www.odod.state.oh.us/onestop/index/ cfm**). This particular site is helpful because it offers step-by-step advice and instructions on creating your business. The business information kit includes forms, state regulations and other tools to help answer questions of business entrepreneurs in Ohio. Each state offers similar advice and information kits for entrepreneurs starting business operations in the state. Other resources you can contact for assistance and to gather information is your local Economic Development Center, The Chamber of Commerce or the Small Business Development Center. Call your local Equal Employment Opportunity Commission (EEOC) office as well, so you stay in compliance with any requirements they place on your business. For additional information and to locate local offices, visit **www.eeoc.gov**.

Your state's registration process

Contact your secretary of state's office to learn about the state requirements you have to meet for your business. This office will provide you with the laws with which you must comply in establishing and operating your business. The fee to register your business will vary by state. One of the main functions of the state office is to check to see if the business name you have selected is available or is already in use by another business operating in the state. Some states require you to file for and publish a fictitious name with the local newspaper before officially registering the name. Usually on an annual basis, the state requires you to renew the business name, but renewal times vary by state.

The state's department of taxation office can provide income tax information you need to be aware of for your business. This department supplies the necessary forms, tax tables, filing requirements, and publications to help you understand and meet tax-filing deadlines for the business. This information includes payroll deposit requirements for federal and state taxes, as determined by the type of your business, as well as federal and state unemployment deposit amounts and deadlines. Missing or not adhering to deadlines can earn your business expensive penalties, fines, and interest.

City business license

In most cities across the United States, you will need to register the business with the city where it operates. The city supplies a business license, which permits you to operate the business within the city limits. The county where your headquarters is may also require a business license. If you work with clients in various cities, you may need to obtain a license in each of the cities where you have business before conducting business there. The fees associated with obtaining your business license vary by location. You can contact your local chamber of commerce to obtain the requirements and information you need to obtain your business license. If you are taking over an existing coaching firm, most states require that you apply for a license in your own name.

Sales tax

Many states charge and collect sales tax on goods and services purchased for retail use by the consumer. Some states also collect taxes or tax services a business charges its clients If you have an accountant, be sure you consult with him or her and your state's Department of Revenue for sales and tax collection to ensure your coaching business is in compliance. Each state's laws on the taxation of a sale are different, but you may need to obtain a vendor's license to collect sales tax, while other states may not require you to collect and pay sales tax at all. Sales taxes can be collected at the city, county, and state levels. The best place to find out what the sales tax requirements are for your business is to contact your state's department of taxation. The office and your state's website provide a variety of helpful resources. Some states require you to post a deposit on bond against possible future tax obligations; however, this may be waived if they require you to post a surety bond, which requires you to pay 5 percent of the total bond amount, from your insurance company instead. Your accountant and financial advisor can also advise you on the requirements your business has to meet.

OTHER LOCAL LICENSES AND REQUIREMENTS

Because each coaching business is unique or caters to a specific niche or industry, there may be other requirements you have to take care of before opening your business to the public.

Fire department

Another permit you need to be aware of is a fire permit. Typically, businesses with a location outside of the home are required to pass a fire safety inspection; however, even home-based coaching businesses that have special equipment or tools of the trade may be required to pass a fire inspection and obtain a fire permit. Contact your local fire department to see what the requirements are.

If you determine you have to undergo a fire inspection, the fire inspector will check your location's fire exits, fire extinguishers, smoke detectors, and sprinkler systems as they pertain to your business. They will evaluate the size of the location and the number of exits to determine the maximum capacity of the location, as necessary. You must follow any guidelines they set in place for your location because failure to do so may result in fines, penalties, or the loss of your fire permit and ability to run your business in the location.

Construction and building

If you are going to remodel or build on your business's location, you are required to obtain a building permit before the construction work can begin. You can obtain building permits from your local building and zoning office (usually located in city hall). The building inspector may require a copy of your building or remodeling plans and require the building to undergo an inspection before, during, and after the building commences. The final inspection of the building project includes a safety inspection of the footers, framing, insulation, electrical, plumbing, and other important elements of the building construction. You may also need to comply with appearance guidelines according to local requirements. Some cities require buildings to use some materials or approval of paint colors before the building is finished.

Sign permits

Some areas have laws to regulate the use of signs on buildings or on the street where the business is located. Signage requirements may cover the type, size, location, and lighting of the business sign you want to use for your business. According to county regulations and even the building regulations where your business is located, there are various sign requirements, including how high the sign can stand, how close to the business, and how close to the street it is. Before purchasing any type of sign for your business, check the city, county, and community codes where your business operates. For example, if placeing a sign for your coaching business on the front lawn of your home, you may be charged a hefty fine for placing the sign in a residential community that does not permit business signs.

Zoning requirements

An area's zoning requirements dictate how buildings located in the zone can be used. For example, residential zoning allows for living while commercial zoning permits businesses to run out the location. Working out of your home is not typically affected by these zoning requirements, but check with your county permit department because some counties require you to obtain a home office permit. Some of the aspects of your business that can be affected by zoning requirements are where you can operate the business, where clients can park, and even what type of vehicles you can have in your driveway.

Employee identification number (EIN)

Even if you are a sole proprietor, you may wish to obtain an employee identification number (EIN) for your business, so you do not have to give your social security number to clients and vendors for income tax reporting purposes. If you are an employer, partnership, or a corporation, the IRS requires you to obtain an EIN for your business. This is the equivalent to a social security number but is used when filing your business tax forms, to open a business bank account, and to establish credit accounts for the business.

The process for obtaining an EIN for your business is relatively simple. The IRS's online application walks you through the process of requesting the number, which includes completing an application. You can choose to obtain the number via e-mail or regular mail. You also have the option of downloading, printing and completing a paper application directly from **www.irs.gov** or request a paper form be mailed to you. Finally, you can contact the IRS via phone and an IRS agent can process your application by phone.

Registering trademarks

When you use a word, phrase, symbol, or design that is special to your business, and you do not want another company to be able to use it, you can trademark the word, phrase, symbol, or design. You should only trademark items that in some way distinguish your company from any other business. The interesting thing about trademarks is that registering does not create your trademark: public use does. So, you are not required to file a trademark application with the United States Patent and Trademark Office in order to stake claim to the trademarked item. You can simply indicate your claim to the public by using the "TM" (trademark) symbol, which looks like this ™.

When and if you are ready to file a trademark application, you have a couple of different options on how to go about doing it. Your first option to complete the application online using the USPTO's Trademark Electronic Application System (TEAS) at **www.uspto.gov/teas**. This system allows you to complete and submit the trademark application directly over the Internet. You can also use the automated telephone line at 1-800-786-9199 to request a printed application. If you request a paper application, you must submit the application via regular mail or in person in the Alexandria, Virginia office only.

Once you have your business structure in place and have obtained all of the necessary licenses and permits you are ready and able to open for business. Once you are open for business you have to learn how to properly manage your business revenue and expenses in order to run a profitable and successful coaching business.

CHECKLIST

✓ Decide which legal business structure is most beneficial to your business.

✓ Apply for and obtain any special permits or licenses you need in the state, county, and city where the business is located.

✓ Choose and register a business name and trademarks.

✓ Obtain a business or occupational license to operate your coaching business.

✓ Request and obtain an employer identification number (EIN).

Chapter 7: Managing Revenue and Expenses

In this chapter, you will:

- Learn how to make projections on the revenue and expenses of the business.

- Discover bookkeeping and spending strategies to help create a profitable and legally compliant business.

- Uncover the secret ways you can keep expenses at a minimum, especially for the first few years of the business, until it starts to turn a profit.

Your business is well on its way to getting started, and you may already have landed a client or two. You are ready to jump right into the world of coaching, but managing your business is equally important as the coaching work. The big obstacle that many coaching businesses face is how to set up their business bookkeeping or accounting records in an organized and efficient manner. Unfortunately, this is one aspect of getting your business up and running that can be one of the most difficult to organize. For this reason, spending time to learn how to handle the financial records of the business now can save you from a messy situation in the future.

THE BUSINESS BUDGET

Although your business plan includes a written estimate of your business budget you can use as a starting point, your business' life involves managing the budget you have put in place. Internal bookkeeping practices are an essential part of success to run business, and all financial transactions need to be recorded, reviewed, and balanced.

For coaches who are not mathematically inclined, it may behoove you to hire a professional accountant to handle these details of your business. When your business is first starting out, you can probably work with an accountant on a part-time basis. If you do decide to outsource this function, you still need to stay involved so you know and understand every financial detail as it pertains to your business's financial health. The faster potential problems are brought to light, the faster you can get these issues corrected and under control.

If you decide to be the financial manager of your own business, it may take you several hours daily (or at least weekly) to focus on and manage your business accounting. Luckily, accounting software programs are available and can be a helpful tool for keeping track of your books. It is still wise to have an accountant review your financial records on a quarterly basis to check for accuracy and offer advice on any adjustments to make.

Accounting software

One of the best tools available to anyone starting their own business is accounting software. There are many types available, though some are better suited to different types of coaching businesses than others are. Nonetheless, the benefits of investing in the accounting software can far outweigh the cost of purchasing and implementing it.

One of the most popular is Intuit QuickBooks® accounting software, which is specifically designed as a package with resources for small businesses. QuickBooks can help you with everything from managing inventory to keeping your profit and loss statement up-to-date. For certain business structures, QuickBooks even allows for electronic filing of the business federal tax returns. You can buy this in most office supply and computer software stores, as well as online on websites such as **www.quickbooks. com**. Pricing on the software starts at $99.95 for the most basic version and goes up to $600 for the most comprehensive versions, with enhanced reporting for up to three users and QuickBooks support service.

Another popular accounting software is Peachtree (**www.peachtree.com**) by Sage Accounting Software, which offers many benefits and features to you as a small business owner. Peachtree offers different versions of the software, so you can find the version that is right for your business. For one to five users, the first three versions (Peachtree Pro, Peachtree Complete, and Peachtree Premium) are available. Peachtree Quantum is the only version that allows more than five users. All versions offer standard accounting and management tools. The complete version also offers advanced inventory, job costing, an audit trail, and fixed assets tools. The premium version offers serialized inventory, Crystal Reports®, and advanced budgeting tools. Prices range from $199.99 to $12,000, depending on the version and number of users that can access the software.

These are but two of the many accounting software programs on the market. You can view and compare different software options at **www.2020software. com**. The site lists the 20 top-rated accounting software programs, shows side-by-side comparisons of the various options, offers free demos, and you can speak with an accounting software specialist for additional help.

Payroll planning

If your coaching business has employees, or if you are the employee, it helps to understand the inner working of the payroll system of your business. In most cases, the process is simple for a one-coach business, but in the case where there are multiple employees it is a more complicated process.

Bookkeepers can do payroll for your business by cutting the employee paychecks, making the required tax withholding deposits, and filing all of the necessary paperwork. Accounting software programs such as QuickBooks (**www.quickbooks.intuit.com**) or Sage Peachtree (**www.peachtree.com**) also offer payroll features, which automates much of this work for you. A third option is to hire a professional payroll service to handle your payroll needs. In any of these situations, you will need to have a daily report prepared containing your daily accounts so you can provide employee information to your payroll accounting service for tracking data such as the salary or wages paid, deduction amounts for social security and Medicare taxes, and the number of hours worked if an hourly employee.

If you wish to allocate the time, your payroll service, bookkeeper, or accounting software program can do this for you as well. You can define the categories and the hours spent on each client. This is especially helpful when you are charging clients on an hourly basis because clients want to see what they received for the fee they paid. Either way, you can use this daily checklist to make sure your bookkeeping function is completed daily.

CHECKLIST

- ✓ Gather the number of hours worked by each employee (preferably as a written timecard).

- ✓ Verify the hours match the amount of time the employees worked.

- ✓ Record hours on payroll software or report it to your payroll service or bookkeeper.

- ✓ Determine the gross amount to be paid to each employee.

- ✓ For salaried employees, divide the employee's monthly salary by the number of days worked in the month (or divide the annual salary by 52 to determine a weekly salary amount).

- ✓ Total up the gross amounts for each day.

At the end of the week, total each employee's gross pay (your accounting software should do this for you). All records should be checked for accuracy. For example, if your two employees are working with a large client and you pay them hourly, you need to keep track of the hours the employees work to pay them and to track how much to charge the client. Preparing these figures on a daily basis helps you stay up to date on where your business stands financially. Reconciling this information with your budget can help you keep your business afloat.

Handling taxes

When it comes to dealing with business taxes, coaching businesses need to pay special attention to keeping accurate and up-to-date business records. Because coaching is typically a service business, it is more difficult for the IRS to track sales and expenses than it is for a product-based business. Therefore, the IRS is more likely to monitor service businesses in an effort to avoid tax fraud, so it is imperative to keep accurate records. One of the biggest issues with business taxes is determining how much you need to pay. With the various types of county, state, and federal taxes your business may be responsible for paying, there is no one calculation that applies to every business. One of the best places to start to get a handle on your business taxes is with the IRS; its website provides a myriad of information on resources on almost any tax matter you can think of occurring.

When it comes to federal business taxes, the three main categories you need to be concerned with paying and filing the appropriate forms are:

1. Income tax withheld from employees wages or from non-payroll amounts.

2. Social security and Medicare taxes (FICA taxes) from each employees' wages and the social security and Medicare taxes you pay as an employer.

3. Federal unemployment (FUTA) tax.

If you do not have any employees you may not have to worry about pay these taxes. Talk with your accountant or contact the IRS to determine if these taxes are applicable to your business. To file your business tax return, you may need access to the following forms:

Form 940 (or 940-EZ), Employer's Annual Federal Unemployment (FUTA) Tax Return: This form is due one month after the calendar year ends. Use it to report your FUTR tax. Most employers can use Form 940-EZ. Go to the IRS website (**www.irs.gov/pub/irs-pdf/f940.pdf**) to acquire the form.

Form 941, Employer's Quarterly Federal Tax Return: File this one month after the calendar month or quarter ends. (The amounts of your payments dictate how often you need to file.) This form is used to report social security, Medicare, and federal income taxes withheld on your employees' wages. Go to the IRS website (**www.apps2.irs.gov/pub/irs-pdf/f941.pdf**) to acquire the exact form.

Managing your cash

As you start working with clients, cash flow management comes into play. Your cash flow is the amount of money your company earns and spends during a certain time, and for your business to break even, you need to have enough cash flow to pay for bills, supplies and other business expenses.

Managing your business cash flow accurately is crucial to running a successful business. It is good business practice for you to stay on top of your bills, so you always pay them on time. Doing so can often save you money, as some suppliers discount the amount you owe when you pay early or on time. Paying bills late, on the other hand, can cost you more because you will be assessed late fees and finance charges on top of the amount you owe. In some situations, you will develop working relationships with suppliers and other vendors, which may afford you a 30-day window to pay your bill. This window allows you to leverage your cash flow, especially if your cash flow fluctuates during the month.

Managing cash flow comes down to inputting the payments you receive from clients into your accounting software as well as tracking the payments you are dispensing. It is similar to keeping a check register for your personal checking account. When you make a deposit, you place the deposit amount in the income column and add it to the total balance in your account. When you write a check, use your debit card, or withdraw cash from the account, you subtract the amount of money going out of the account from the balance. You keep track of the income and expenses going in and out of the account so you know how much money you have to spend and how much money you may need to earn to cover upcoming expenses. The same concept holds true for managing the cash flow in your coaching business.

Accepting client payments

One of the factors you need to consider is the types of payments you will accept from clients. You can choose to accept cash, checks, money orders, cashier's checks, debt, and credit cards. Determining which type of payments you accept from clients also affects your cash flow. For example, if you choose to accept only checks then you simply have to cash or deposit the check into your business bank account. You will only be charged fees on the check if it bounces for some reason.

There are a couple of disadvantages to accepting checks. First, you have to wait to receive the check from the client, either in person or by mail. This can cause a delay in your receipt of the payment. Second, you have to make a trip to the bank to deposit it into your account, and if the check is from an out-of-state bank or over the bank's limit amount, the funds may be put on hold, which means you will not have immediate access to the money. Third, if the check bounces because the client does not have sufficient funds in his or her bank account, your bank may charge bounced check fees; this may even cause checks you have written from your bank account to bounce, which can result in even more bounced check fees for you to pay.

If you choose to accept credit cards, on the other hand, you are typically charged a percentage of the transaction as a fee. The percentages can range from two percent of the transaction amount to more than 3 percent. There are typically transaction fees as well, so each time you run a credit card for payment, not only are you charged the percentage of the transaction amount, but you also pay a flat rate fee, which can range from 30 cents up. Instead of receiving 100 percent of the client payment, you walk away with the amount left after the credit card processing fee is deducted. Because there are various ways you can receive payments from clients, consider the pros and cons of each option — including the costs — before deciding which forms of payment you should accept for your business. Here are some of the payment options you can consider accepting from clients:

- **Cash**: Be sure to provide the client with a receipt signed by you and the client when you accept this form of payment. A signed receipt is your only record of the transaction.

- **Checks**: Personal or business checks have some risk because they may bounce, but you typically do not pay fees for cashing or depositing checks into your business account. Be sure to charge a fee for any returned checks (and record that fee amount at the time of billing).

- **Credit and debit cards**: Accepting credit and debit payments is convenient, and with instant approval or denial you have a sense of security that the money is available. Clients like to pay with credit cards because it allows clients to pay off the charge down the line.

- **Online**: Online payment-processing programs such as PayPal and Google Checkout allow you to accept credit card or check payments online, which speeds up the payment process. Again, there is a fee for using these services, but it is typically less expensive than having a credit card machine. The fee charged is a percentage of the transaction amount, but typically starts at 1 percent of the transaction amount and goes up to slightly more than 2 percent, depending on the type of credit card the client uses and the account level you have established with PayPal or Google Checkout.

Tips for accepting cash and checks

When using cash, keep these things in mind:

- **Trust the cash collector**: If you are entrusting the collection of cash to someone in your business other than you, it is imperative that the person collecting the cash is reliable and honest. Making one person responsible for collecting and managing the cash makes it easier to track mistakes, mishaps, or theft.

- **Keep detailed records**: All cash transactions should be recorded with details on the exact amount paid, when the cash payment was received and exactly what the payment covers (which services).

- **Generate a cash receipt**: The client and the person in your business accepting the payment should sign this receipt. Include detailed information such as the payment amount, date, and reason for the payment.

- **Balance the cash drawer**: The cash drawer should be balanced on a regular basis and excess amounts should be deposited in the bank. Businesses that have a high amount of cash transaction balance the cash drawer and make deposits on a daily basis. Those with a less cash volume business may only do this once a month

When using checks, keep these things in mind:

- **Include a returned check fee**: In the terms section of the client contract or agreement, spell out the fee that will be charged to clients for any returned checks.

- **Include all contact information for the payee**: On the check, include an address, phone number, and business name (if appropriate). Verify this information for an individual against a picture ID before accepting a check as payment. This information can help to avoid accepting fraudulent checks and help you to track down the client for payment in the event the check bounces or you have some other problem with depositing or cashing the check.

- **Generate a receipt**: Create a receipt for check payments and have the client sign it. Include the amount of the payment, the date of the payment, and the reason for the payment.

- **Consider using a check confirmation system**: These systems verify that there is money available in the account from which the check is written at the time you take the check. The system can place the funds on hold until the check clears. This can be an expensive service, but it can also be beneficial when accepting a check from a client for the first time. Contact your bank for more information on the cost of this system and how to implement it.

Contracts and payments

In the world of coaching, you will find that most clients pay with a check, but you can set the proper payment expectations with the client when the client contracts your services.

Make sure each client contract outlines specific dates or milestones that trigger a payment and how much is due for each payment. Because you will most likely spread the payments out into several stages, your first step is to request an up-front payment or deposit to start the project. This provides you and the client with a sense of security. You know that you are working with a client that has a vested interest, so you do not end up working for free. The client has received assurance that he or she has booked your time and services in advance. It is less likely that a client will walk away when they have given you a deposit or up-front payment.

Collecting payments is a give-and-take situation between you and the client. When you reach certain milestones, the client receives an invoice from you and in return you receive a portion of the total fee. This helps to provide you with a steady revenue flow as you begin working with the client without having to wait until the end to get paid.

With retainer clients or clients you work with on a regular basis, you can set a regular payment schedule where you invoice them on a weekly or monthly basis. Whatever the agreement is, make sure the details are in your contract.

Your budget and operational management

As part of any normal business operation, setting a realistic budget and then sticking to it can make a huge difference in a business succeeding or failing. This requires you to assess your budget situation before making any business purchases or investments. When creating a business budget, two budgets work in conjunction with each other. One deals with short-term expenses such as office supplies and the business phone bill, while the other deals with long-term financial plans for the business such as expanding your office space to accommodate more employees or moving from a home-based office to a rented space.

At least once a year, analyze your business needs to examine the costs associated with running the business. When reviewing your business revenue and expenses, compare the actual amount spent with the amount that was budgeted for at the start. This analysis reveals shortfalls or overspending so you can allocate money into categories of your budget better in the future. When there is a discrepancy between these numbers, find out which factors contributed to the discrepancy. Assessing the budget on a regular basis makes it easier to adjust and accommodate the costs now rather than waiting six months to find out your business is in the hole.

For your short-term budgeting practices, develop a monthly budget for the business. The first month you are in business may be more challenging to calculate costs than the months that follow, and it may take you a couple of months to truly understand what expenses your business has so that you can create a realistic budget. Over time, setting the monthly budget will become easier and most likely more accurate. Creating and using a monthly budget as a guide for your business reveals how much money you can use for various expenses throughout the month. Ultimately, this budget helps you define where your business is going and what adjustments are required to achieve your business goals. Tracking the business budget can also be helpful when and if you apply for a business loan, while also making it possible to meet your business financial goals. Accounting software programs have budgeting tools that allow you to create and keep track of your spending or you can build a spreadsheet (or use a sheet of paper and a pencil) to build and track the business budget.

Choose the way you feel most comfortable in creating and tracking your budget, which boils down to creating a list of expenses and assigning an estimated cost to each expense. Once you list out all of the expenses, you can total them up to see what the total expenses are for the month.

Creating a budget is about estimating these costs; so create a separate column to track the actual cost of each expense. You may also want to create a separate column to record the difference between the estimated and actual cost. In essence, a budget for the month may contain five columns. Column one is the date of the expense, column two is the type of expense (phone service, office rent, or electricity), column three is the estimated cost, column four is the actual cost, and the final column is the difference, if any, between the estimated and actual cost.

Making revenue projections

Not only is it important to track the spending in your business, but it is also equally important to project sales or the revenue stream coming into the business. The best way to do this is to track earnings as you start to do business with client. In addition, it is important to factor in that your earnings will probably be lower when you first start your coaching business, but as time progresses, these earnings should grow. With less money coming into the business and high one-time, start-up expenses in the beginning, you will probably see a lower profit margin for the business and for you. In some situations, you may break even or lose money during the first few months in business. Tracking the profit margin for each service can also play a pivotal role in turning a business profit. Tracking the profit margins on your services helps you to focus on providing those services that are bringing profits to your coaching company.

Part of being in a business is starting off slow and watching the revenues of your business grow over time. Growing your business requires you to project the business revenue and then track it to make sure it is growing rather than declining. If business revenues hit a peak or a plateau, it is imperative that you understand what caused the peak, plateau or plummet so you can make adjustments to either mimic it or improve it. For example, a personal fitness coaching business may hit a peak during the first few months of the year and as the summer months approach because people are trying to fulfill their New Year's resolutions and get in shape for swimsuit season. Another example may be that a special promotion creates a spike in your clients. Understanding what may be causing these swings is important because it pinpoints what is affecting the business profitability.

It is important to continuously track and compare your current revenue month-by-month, quarter-by-quarter, and year-by-year. Review these records often to compare the services, discounts, client base, and any other factors that may contribute to the rise or fall in these numbers.

THE COSTS OF DOING BUSINESS

The costs of doing business can vary greatly from company to company. One type of coaching company may have very little overhead or low expenses, while another coaching company has a huge overhead and more expenses than income. For example, a marketing coach that works out of a home office has very little overhead. A personal training coach that has expensive exercise machines and equipment or has to maintain a membership to a gym to train clients has much more overhead and expenses. As a business owner, you have to track all of your business expenses and revenue. First, you need to know some of the business costs you may run up against so you can factor these costs into your budget. Some of the costs will not apply to your business, while other costs not listed here may apply to your type of coaching business. This is why factoring in a cushion of money into your budget for emergencies and other unexpected expenses is important.

Labor costs

Labor is the cost of hiring employees. This includes everyone from the person selling your services to the person managing your front office. If you have employees, you need to know how much it is costing your business. When labor costs get too high, you can cut back on the number of employees and hire additional help when needed. The number of employees you have on the payroll should be justified by the amount of business being generated from the employees.

Perhaps one of the highest costs in terms of labor is overtime. When you have an employee who works more than 40 hours a week, you end up paying him or her 1 1/2 times the normal pay rate. It is less expensive, in most cases, to hire an additional employee or to outsource the work instead of paying an employee to work overtime.

Controllable operational costs

Controlling business costs, especially when you first start your business is the key to keeping expenses low and helping to make your profit margin higher. With controllable costs, you can either choose to spend money on these costs or not, thus giving you more leeway with your expenses. Even if you decide to spend the money, you can still control how much you spend. Here is a brief look at some of the business expenses you can control:

Large purchases

When you first start a business, there are likely to be larger purchases to acquire the equipment, furniture, and other supplies you need to start. Though a purchase may be necessary, there are ways you can keep these costs down. For example, if you need to purchase a desk for your office, scour second-hand stores, furniture sales, garage sales and Craigslist (**www. craigslist.org**) to find gently used furniture at a deep discount. Another option to keep costs down is to repurpose items you already have to fit your needs. Instead of purchasing a new desk, consider using a table you have until you can afford to purchase a desk or borrow items from friends and family.

Service staples

Even though coaching is a service business, there are supplies you may need to keep on hand. For example, if you are an accounting coach, you may need to acquire accounting software licenses to set up an accounting software program for each of your clients at their office. Because this is a cost for a specific product, you need to factor it in to your costs on an ongoing basis. Office supplies are another category that may fall into the staples category. Everything from printer paper and specialty paper to pens, folders, and paper clips may be required. These are consumables, so you will need to replace them often, but keeping an inventory of office supplies helps reduce costs in the long run. Shop discount office supply stores online, which is less expensive than shopping bigger chain office supply stores — even with shipping.

Services

Your business may require some professional service providers, such as an attorney and accountant, but other services may not be as important. If you cannot afford to hire an accountant or payroll service, then consider lower-cost options such as purchasing and maintaining an accounting software program to help with this aspect of the business. Also think along the lines of your shipping services when cutting costs or trying to keep operational costs to a minimum. For example, if you are sending a client information, decide if you really need to print it out, put it in a company folder, and pay for it to go overnight to the client or if e-mailing the information is an effective, faster, and less expensive way to go.

Maintenance costs

Other operational costs include the maintenance of your office, equipment, company vehicles, and other machines you may own or lease for the business. These costs may include repair costs or fees for the upkeep on the items to keep everything in working order. It is also important to consider that paying for maintenance can save you replacement costs on the equipment, so you do not want to disregard the maintenance altogether.

Utilities

Whether you run your coaching business at another location or in your home, utility costs for water and electricity are necessary operational costs. If you are running the business from its own location, utility costs will probably be higher than the small increase you may see for running your business out of your home. Other utility costs may include telephone and Internet service. You can keep costs down by only subscribing to those services that are necessary to run your business. For example, phone service packages may include many features you do not need. Check with the phone company to see how much you can save if you only have the features you need such as call waiting and voice mail service.

Operating an energy-efficient business also saves money on utility bills. When machines, equipment, and lights are not in use turn them off and unplug them from the power source where applicable. When you close your business for the day, make sure you turn everything off. If you leave your computer for more than ten minutes, place it in sleep mode or set it up so that it automatically goes into sleep mode after a specified amount of time.

Fixed operating costs

Though you may be able to control the amount you spend on some operational costs, other costs of running your coaching business are fixed costs, which mean the costs do not change from one payment cycle to the next. Fixed costs are also included as part of your business operational budget and can be easier to manage since the cost does not change.

Rent/mortgage

Whether you rent or own the property where you run your business, your rent or mortgage payment is the same month after month. This will be one of the first fixed costs that you will want to pay each month to ensure you have a location to run your business.

Insurance costs

Liability insurance is a necessity when running a coaching business, so at the very least your insurance fixed cost covers this type of coverage. Depending on where your business location is (in or out of your home) you may have other insurance costs. Typically, insurance payments remain the same for long periods of time. Liability, theft, fire, and worker's compensation are a few types of insurance you may want to consider or may be required by law to obtain. Theft and fire insurance cover you in the event you lose the ability to run your office because of burglary or fire damage. Some policies offer you coverage for establishing a temporary office, while others only cover you for returning your existing office to its original condition. If you have employees on staff, worker's compensation can protect you in case of an employee injury. The insurance covers the cost of the employee's medical needs and can also protect you by paying the damages from a lawsuit brought on by the employee.

Property taxes

Property tax is another fixed cost that tends to come due once a year. If you are running your business out of your home, this should not affect the cost of your taxes. If you own a business location outside of your home, the county assesses a property tax value that you must pay at least once a year.

Miscellaneous costs

Other costs you need to consider and be aware of for running your coaching business include:

Labor taxes

If, or when, you have employees on the payroll you will be responsible for paying taxes to the state and federal governments. Paying labor taxes requires you to establish an account with your business banking institution to deposit withholding amounts for each payroll period. These taxes typically include state and federal unemployment and social security.

Repair costs

Repairs for equipment, a company vehicle, or office location are unexpected costs that you may have to manage as well. Because these are unexpected expenses, keep a cushion of extra cash on hand to cover repair costs.

Client entertainment

You will be working with clients, so there will be times when you need to woo them with a nice lunch, dinner, or tickets to the local sports game. Build some money into your budget to cover these types of client entertainment expenses and keep track of your spending because most of these items are tax deductible.

Advertising

Marketing and promoting your business typically requires quite a bit of your business budget — especially when you first launch the business. *Once you complete your marketing plan in Chapter 10, you will have a better grasp on how much marketing expenses can be.* Remember though, if nobody knows your business exists then it is going to be very difficult to attract clients and extremely difficult to stay in business.

Fees

Many coaching businesses have to pay trade dues or business association fees, which also needs to be taken into consideration when building your business budget. Also, the fees for obtaining and renewing the necessary business and occupational licenses should be allotted to this portion of your budget.

Client costs

Times when you need to travel to visit or meet with a client, or you need to book a meeting room are other types of costs that need to be considered. When possible, costs of this nature should be paid by the client and established in your written agreement, but you may initially need the cash on hand to cover the costs until receiving reimbursement from the client.

Bad debt

Although you may do everything in your power to avoid it, there are times when a client simply goes bad or takes a wrong turn. A client may disappear on you without paying you everything they owe, or you may underestimate a time frame so working with the client ends up costing more than you are earning. These types of instances are losses to your company that adversely affect your profit margin. Some of these losses may be tax deductible, but some come directly out of your budget, so keep track of these losses. For example, the interest you pay on business credit card balances is not a tax-deductible debt. If you carry large credit card balances, you are most likely paying interest that reaches into the double digits, and all of the interest you are paying is an added expense that you cannot write-off as a business expense at the end of the year.

Calculating profit or loss

Once you keep a running tab of your income and your expenses, it is pretty easy to calculate your profit (or loss). Using all of the figures — keeping track of costs, expenses, and client payments — you simply subtract all of your costs and expenses from the total amount of money your services have brought into the company (revenue). When you subtract your expenses from your income, if the number is positive, then you have a profit. When you subtract your expenses from your income, if the number is negative then you have a loss. If and when you have a profit, decide how much of the company profit you will use to pay yourself a salary as opposed to how much of the profit will be reinvested back into the business. For example, assume you are calculating profit and loss for the month of February, and the total monthly expenses are $2,575 with the total monthly income reaching $5,250.

Monthly profit: $5,250 – $2,575 = $2,675

In cases where the number is positive, this indicates a profit (more money was made than was spent). If the answer of the calculation is a negative number, this indicates a loss (more money was spent than was made).

CHECKLIST

✓ Project and create a budget on expected revenue and expenses for the business.

✓ Research the possibilities of how you will handle your business financials.

✓ Build in cost-saving measures while building your budget but also create a cushion for emergencies and unexpected expenses.

✓ Track all of your revenue and expenses, and calculate whether your business is operating at a profit or loss.

Chapter 8:
How to Manage Your
Time and Yourself

In this chapter, you will:

- Learn time management skills and tips on how to make the best use of your time.

- Discover how to balance your time so that you devote enough time to being a business owner, as well as handling client projects.

- Decide when and if it is time to delegate certain aspects of the business to others.

One of the primary skills of running a successful coaching business goes beyond your knowledge and experience in the industry or niche you serve. You also have to learn how to be a business owner. Finding the right balance in devoting time to your role as a business owner and as a coach can be challenging because both roles can be full-time jobs. Finding the balance really comes down to learning how to effectively manage your time, which also entails learning how to manage yourself in the process.

TIME IS MONEY

As a business owner, you no longer have a boss to monitor your time and task completion because you are the boss. In fact, there is no one looking over your shoulder to keep you on schedule or to make sure the company is heading toward achieving its goals. You are in charge, which means you are the only one accountable for the hours you work and for the work getting done. For most coaches who are also business owners, this is the most difficult challenge they have to overcome.

Though you have the ability to spend countless hours at your desk working away or decide to call it a day at 2 p.m., the first thing you have to realize is that time is money. By learning to manage your time, you can also effectively manage your income while delivering the high quality service you want to provide to your clients (and the paycheck to match all of your efforts). If you are not able to organize and manage your time effectively, you may end up wasting precious time, which also equates to wasting money before you have an opportunity to earn it.

Managing your time wisely

Setting priorities is the first step in learning how to manage your time wisely. Every client thinks that his or her issue is more pressing or more important than one of the other clients you are working with. Do not look to your clients to guide you on what to set as a priority over something else. You have to define what your priorities are, even if it means telling a client — in the nicest way possible — that you are unable to deal with their problem right now because you have something else you have to do. If you allow others to control your priorities, you end up not completing the important items, which over time can lead to a loss of business, money, and time.

As a coach, you will have what may be or what seems like an endless demand for your attention. You have to balance meeting the demands of your clients to keep them happy with performing revenue-generating tasks to turn a profit. When setting your priorities for the day, there are several things to consider. Once you take these items in consideration, it will become much clearer on the order your tasks should fall.

1. Is the task profitable? Tasks that generate the most revenue for your business directly or indirectly are priorities. The bigger the payoff is, the higher the task should be on your list. For example, if you have the choice of working on your marketing plan or heading out to the store to buy the latest smart phone, then working on your marketing plan should take priority. Though putting together a marketing plan may not make you $1,000 today, it is a task that can make your company more profitable over time. On the contrary, tasks that have less of an impact on your profitability should be toward the bottom of your task list, such as administrative tasks like filing or tackling long-term projects like redesigning your coaching business website.

2. Is it something you should handle or delegate to someone else? Many business owners get caught up in the fact that they are the only ones that can do something right, so they may as well handle everything. Highly effective and successful people quickly learn that the true way to make it to the top is to build a great support team, either as employees or as independent contractors. This allows the business owner

to focus on profit-generating activities and delegate tasks that someone else has the ability to handle. Delegation can propel you toward meeting your business goals faster than getting bogged down with everything and getting nothing accomplished in the process.

3. Are you the emergency room doctor? What clients often think is an emergency and what is truly an emergency typically are two different things. As the emergency room doctor, it is up to you to decide. If it is a real problem that needs handling immediately, then move it toward the top of your priority list. Build some time into your daily schedule in case emergencies arise so it does not completely throw off your entire schedule.

As projects come in, use the three-step approach listed above to determine the priority level of the project. As you complete a project, move to the next top priority on your list. Some days you will get through your entire list. Other days, you may not get past the first item on your task list. Continue to plan each day using your list, rearranging items in order of importance. Prioritize your list for the day according to the deadlines that need to be met for each task.

Eight effective time-management tips

Managing your time and your effectiveness starts with knowing what your goals are and how to meet them. These eight tips will help you to get on the right track to managing your time.

Tip 1: Always be in the know

The first place to start is with a list of projects and tasks that need to be tackled. Although these items may not be in order just yet, you always need to know what needs to be done and have a big-picture view. You must always have all of the information you need at your fingertips; therefore, you must always be organized. If you work best with a hard-copy day planner that you carry around, then use this as your task system. If a computerized calendar or spreadsheet of projects and tasks is what works to keep you organized, then use this system to keep track of everything. Find an organizational system that works for you, and then learn how to manage it rather than allow it to manage you.

Tip 2: Start off the day right

Each morning when you start your workday, pull out your schedule/task list or pull up your goals on the computer. Your tasks should be in order of priority, so you can start to tackle the most important item on your list and work your way down the list as you complete each task. As you progress through the day, you will also find yourself adding items to your list. Work these items in according to priority. If the task is more important than an item already on the list, then insert the new item above the existing items that are less important. If the new item is less important, add it to the bottom of the list.

Tip 3: End the day right

At the end of each workday, set some time aside to prepare and organize the schedule for the following day. Review the current day's task list, and assess what you were able to accomplish and what items on the list need to be moved to the following day. Prepare the plan, task list, and schedule for the following day, so you are ready to get started right away. It may also be beneficial to save administrative tasks such as invoicing and filing for the end of the day because this is the time when you are typically winding down or getting tired. Clean off your desk so it is fresh and clean when you arrive tomorrow, turn off your lights and computer, and end your workday on an organized note.

Tip 4: Tackle your first priority first

Make sure that you are handling your daily tasks according to its priority status. It may sound simple, but the first priority is often a difficult task or project, so coaches tend to avoid handling it and instead focus on smaller, less difficult, and less important tasks. Coaches often rationalize that getting all of the little things off their plate allows them to focus on what is important. The opposite, however, ends up being the case. Yes, all of the smaller items may be crossed off the list, but the priority item is still staring them in the face — unaccomplished and incomplete. Projects with looming deadlines, matters with a sense of urgency, and problems need to be handled first. After that, you can focus on less important items.

If the task list has 25 items on it, you probably are not going to accomplish everything on your list in one day. Realize that it is acceptable to not accomplish everything on your list in one day. As long as you have set your priorities correctly, you will have accomplished the tasks with the utmost of importance.

Tip 5: Cut out tasks that are not lucrative

Focus your efforts for the bulk of the day on tasks that are lucrative and make the coaching business money. This includes marketing tasks, coaching clients, and preparing proposals for new clients. Checking and responding to e-mails, filing, and playing with the calendar are less lucrative tasks. These are tasks that need to be done, so schedule a set time to tackle these tasks and then stick to your schedule. The more time you spend on activities that do not generate income, the less time you have for finding new clients, working on meeting deadlines, and making money. Instead of reading blogs for the first hour of your workday, spend that time networking to find your next client, and save blog reading for the end of the day.

It can also be helpful to filter e-mail coming in through your e-mail system so that specific client e-mails are easily accessible, and all of the spam and promotional e-mails are placed in a folder that you can access at a more convenient time, if ever.

Tip 6: Use your time wisely

As a coach, there may be down time throughout the day when you are not working with a client or attempting to complete a lucrative task. Other down times include waiting at the airport to catch a flight to meet with a client or sitting in the taxi on the way to the airport. Rather than let these times go to waste, take along work that can be completed during the ride in the cab, sitting in the airport terminal, and while on the airplane. Networking opportunities may also present themselves during travel of this nature, so talk to the people sitting around you at the airport and on the plane and hand out business cards when appropriate. You never know where your next client may be.

Tip 7: Technology is your friend

Technology can be a useful and helpful tool for a coaching business because it allows you to make wise use of time. Because time is money, properly utilizing technology can be very lucrative for a coaching business. Using an iPhone®, BlackBerry, or another smart phone can help consolidate your technological needs into one instrument. These devices are a phone, calendar, e-mail system, word processing system, and task creator, all wrapped up in one convenient package — and with Internet access.

Investing in a laptop rather than a desktop computer may be a wiser option for coaches that are always on the go rather than always in the office. Software programs are available for coaches to maximize their time by handling certain administrative tasks. E-mail correspondence can replace the cost of physical mail or long distance phone charges. Instant messaging conversations can also replace other forms of communication as a fast, easy, and cost-effective way to get things done. Use the business website to automatically gather business leads. Technology is a coach's most powerful tool, making your business better and helping you grow the bottom line.

Tip 8: Build a cushion of time

When planning a schedule, try not to plan out a task for every minute of the day. Though it is good to have tasks scheduled, everyone needs a break. Take a 15-minute break in the morning and afternoon, and be sure to take time for lunch, too. One coach that works from home eats her lunch and then takes her dog for a quick 20-minute walk around the block. It helps clear her head and exercise the dog at the same time. When she returns to her desk, she has a clearer view of the work before her.

When the afternoon laziness sets in, work on activities that do not require too much brainpower or tackle administrative work. Building in a cushion of time also helps when urgent matters arise because it allows you to allocate what may have been some down time to resolving the problem without having to take too much time away from your other priorities. Time management is one of the most beneficial skills a coach can have. It builds a thriving business, saves you from having to work hard to keep your head above water, and is a completely free tool.

CREATE AN ACTION PLAN

Professional service providers, with coaches being at the top of the list, have to possess or learn organizational skills to run a successful business. Organization is required, not optional, in the coaching industry. Being organized goes beyond knowing where you put a client contract or where the invoice is that you need to send to a client. Being organized is having the ability to find everything you need quickly and efficiently. Organization helps you to manage clutter and easily reach for what you need, but is also an effective tool for managing your stress level.

You may not realize it, but a messy desk or office is counterproductive — even if you are not a neat freak. A messy desk is likely to have sticky notes, piles of paper, and other unnecessary or unused junk. The phone rings and a client asks a question that requires you to find one piece of paper in a stack of hundreds of sheets. As you rummage through the stacks of paper on your desk trying to find the said piece of paper, it is easy for the client to see that you are distracted or cannot put your finger on it. In addition to seeming unprofessional, clutter and disorganization make you feel less in control. Choose an organizational system you like and that works for you and then stick to it.

Getting the office organized and establishing a business system takes a commitment and some of your time. You may want to set aside one full day, or at least a couple of hours, to organize and get your business system in place before you launch your business. Once you establish the organizational system, maintaining it requires your commitment and dedication too, but maintaining an established system is much easier than the initial setup.

- **Start with the desk:** It is easy for a work desk to become crowded with papers, documents, and other office supplies. The good news is that a desk can quickly be cleaned and stay that way. First, throw away (or recycle) any unused items and remove non-work related items from the desk. If you maintain paper files, find a filing cabinet and set up a filing system for invoices, contracts, expenses, long-term clients, and other business needs. Every piece of paper should have a home, and the desk surface is not a home. The surface of the desk and desk drawers should be clean, organized, and contain business items only.

- **Analyze the layout of the office:** Even an office of a couple hundred square feet can have an efficient, organized, and clean setup. Whether your office is your guest bedroom or a section of the dining room, analyze the space available as well as the furniture and equipment that must be present in the space. After removing anything from the space that is not business related or necessary, arrange everything so it fits comfortably and is appealing to look at and work in. Rearrange everything until all necessary items have a home.

- **Scheduling time and appointments:** Everyone uses different techniques to keep track of a calendar and schedule. Whatever system works best for you, keep it close enough to your phone so you can make notes as clients call you or you call them to schedule appointments. Always put everything directly and immediately into the calendar to help meet deadlines and stay on top of appointments, meetings, and tasks. The next section of this chapter goes into more detail on the different calendar management systems you can use and the pros and cons of each system.

- **Go as paperless as possible:** An amazing thing about using your computer to manage as much of running the coaching business as possible is it can also reduce a major amount of paper clutter. Keep business files, invoices, and contracts on your computer. E-mail items instead of printing them out. You can even use a digital signature to sign documents and contracts before sending them to a client, so there is no need to print it out, sign it, fax it, and then have to worry about creating a file to house it. You can even turn hard-copy paperwork into digital files by scanning and storing the document on the computer filing system and then shred or recycle the original document. It is easy to accomplish a computer filing system with a program like Microsoft Word, where a file is created for each client and everything that pertains to the client can go in the file. Electronic files eliminates stacks of paperwork from building up on the desk, avoids making a mess, instantly files the document away in its place, is easy to access again when you need it, and is, above all, organized. Use an online backup system or back up files on a CD in case your computer fails.

- **Do it now rather than save it for later:** Once the office is clean and organized, it is time to implement one final strategy of the organizational system: Anything that can be accomplished and put away now should be done immediately rather than setting it aside, creating clutter, and creating a mess. When you receive a piece of paper, do what you need to do with it and then put it in its place. When you pull out a project to work on, put it away before moving on to the next project. When you get into this habit, it becomes part of doing business and helps keep the organizational system up and running.

Manage your schedule

One of the primary benefits of managing time effectively is that managing your calendar and schedule pushes your business forward. Having a time-management system in place propels the coaching business forward. A lack of a scheduling system can be a hindrance and hold the coaching business back from success.

As mentioned in the previous section, there are several scheduling options available that range from basic to more advanced options. Selecting the most appropriate system depends on the type of coaching business, technology budget, and personal preferences you have. Here is a closer look at a few options, along with the pros and cons for each system:

The calendar

The simplest method available for scheduling is the written paper calendar. Whether a wall, desk, or other type of calendar, it is easy to use, inexpensive, and does the job of keeping track of appointments, meetings, and important dates. Use a pencil so items can easily be erased, rearranged, or changed. The biggest downfall of a wall or desk calendar is that it is not portable, so it cannot easily be put in a briefcase or purse and pulled out to consult when communicating with clients when you are on the go. Another drawback is that paper calendars have space limitations, so it is difficult to write everything in the space available.

Day planners

A day planner is a step up from a calendar because day planners tend to be portable, depending on the style and size. Additionally, day planners provide advanced options for organization, using a tabbing system to separate months as well as to divide the calendar portion from the address book and other sections that typically come in a day planner. Some day planners even have compartments for housing small papers, business cards, and paperclips. Some of the other benefits to using day planners come with some of the sections included in the day planner, including places for lists, notes, expense sheets, and car mileage records. Some day planners also have a section for keeping addresses and phone numbers, or even a calculator.

One of the major drawbacks of a day planner is that everything is written: appointments, tasks, contact information, and other records. Another problem is having to carry your day planner, which can become heavy with all of the paper inside of it. It can also be risky to keep personal and professional information stored in a single place because if you lose it, you lose your entire system, from your calendar to all of your contact information.

Electronic systems

Another way to organize schedules, contacts, and notes is with an electronic system. The computer, a personal digital assistant (PDA), and cell phone are all electronic options for tracking the same information as a day planner. From using free calendar and contact systems online to synching your portable electronic device with your computer, the options are almost endless and extremely convenient.

One advantage to an electronic system is that you can easily back it up, so you always have backup files. Another advantage is that you can share your calendar and other information with virtual assistants, employees of the coaching firm, vendors, clients, and anyone else you choose to give access to this information. Finally, electronic systems typically come with everything you need to manage your office from one device, including a calendar, task list, notes section, contact management system, e-mail, and Internet access.

The main drawback of using an electronic system can be the cost. If you do not already own a computer, software, or smart phone, then you may have to purchase one or more of these items to get started. Computerized scheduling can do anything you need it to; consider the cost and how it fits into your budget so you can invest in features and software products you need that are also affordable. On the other hand, it is easy to argue that electronic systems can save so much time that this supersedes the cost.

BUSINESS MANAGER ROLE

As a "solopreneur" coach, you not only play the role of the worker bee, but you also have the responsibility of managing the business. Managing a business requires a changing of roles throughout the day. One minute you may need to be the secretary, and the next minute you are the bookkeeper paying the company bills and vendors. In between it all, the coaching work also has to be handled. Essentially, a business manager is responsible for every task that it takes to make sure the business is operating according to plan. The role includes a wide range of responsibilities that stretch from customer service to making sure that all of the bills are getting paid — even if this simply means that the accountant is receiving a copy of invoices and bills that need to be paid.

So, how can you manage both sides of the business effectively and without completely losing your mind? The answer is that it all comes back to learning how to manage your time wisely and effectively. Divide the day up into coaching work and business tasks. Though the coaching work is what brings money into the business, dealing with the administrative task of sending out invoices also brings money into the business. When creating a daily schedule, schedule time in to handle both sides of the company: coaching and business management.

Delegating responsibilities

At some point, as your business grows, it will come to a point when managing all of the tasks on your own is counterproductive. For some coaching companies, this happens right from the beginning. Other coaching companies expand into the need to either hire additional employees or outsource work that can be delegated.

For most home-based coaches, building a virtual support team is the answer. This allows the owner to delegate roles, responsibilities, and tasks without having to have a full-time staff or renting the office space (and other expenses that come with it). In addition to the cost savings, hiring virtually opens up the pool of talent worldwide because you are not limited to the applicants that are currently living within a driving radius of your business.

If a social media expert is needed to handle your social media marketing campaigns, you can find the best social media expert that you can afford and hire him or her. It does not matter if the expert lives in the Greek Islands and works when he or she wants from the comfort of home. Those expenses remain his or her expenses, and the coaching business expenses remain the coaching business' expenses — minus the fee you have to pay the social media expert for the services, of course.

Experts argue that putting a virtual support team in place when establishing the business is the most beneficial strategy for any small business. It sets the tone for the business by allowing the coach to focus solely on coaching and revenue-generating activities, while each of the virtual support team members focus on what they do best, which also indirectly generates revenue for the business. Virtual roles may include:

- Virtual assistant (VA)

- Social media marketing expert

- Marketing manager

- Public relations manager

- Web designer

- Graphic designer

- Accountant

- Sales manager

- Database manager

- Advertising

CHECKLIST

✓ Decide which time-management and organizational systems to put in place.

✓ Create a daily schedule prioritized by deadlines and project urgency.

✓ Devote a balanced amount of time to coaching work and managing the business.

✓ Determine if you want to start your business by building a virtual support team, or decide at which point in time your business needs to start delegating duties to employees or virtual team members.

Chapter 9:
Building Your Brand

In this chapter, you will:

- Learn how to build a brand around you as the coach, your skills, and your company's unique offering.

- Discover brand building techniques coaches can use both online and offline to build their brand, credibility, and business.

- Create a positioning statement.

- Craft your marketing messaging.

- Discover logo design opportunities and the need (or not) to have a business logo.

- Learn how to create other marketing collateral such as business cards, a website, brochures, and a marketing kit.

- Uncover how to build the marketing foundation for finding and attracting clients to the coaching business.

Building a brand around you as the coach and the specific services provided by the coaching business involves a myriad of factors, including the spirit, personality, slogan, values, look, feel, and benefits the coaching company, its representatives, and its services portray. When building a brand, focus on connecting with the target audience; the brand you build should reflect how you want the target audience to feel when they see your business card, website, or logo. Building a brand is about appealing to all five senses.

To find the brand essence of your company, the next few sections walk you through the process of uncovering the right look and feel, the right brand, for the coaching business. As you go through the steps, also keep in mind that branding flows through to you as the coach and any representatives of your coaching business. In fact, if the coaching business is based on the experience and skills of the coach, which it typically is, then brand building may revolve around the coach because in reality, the coach is the business.

CHARACTER

The first step in the brand process is to determine the character of the company. As a coaching business, how should the business feel and act? What does the business like, and what does it dislike?

A good example of company character is the Walt Disney Company. Disney has created an entire product line, theme parks, and more all based on being the happiest place on earth. Disney's character is fun, whimsical, and magical. This character shines bright in everything Disney does, sells, and supports. From its talking mouse (Mickey Mouse), the Cinderella Castle, and giant teacups to spin around in, fun and whimsical are the overriding theme of everything that has anything to do with Disney.

Branding for a coaching business may be more on the serious side compared to Disney, but maybe not. If a coaching business focuses on coaching actors in their careers, then it is possible that imagination and fantasy trickles into the company brand.

The character of the coaching business is the foundation for the next step in the brand building process, which involves the relationship between the business and its customers: This is customer relations. When a customer purchases an alarm system from a security company, he or she feels safe. When someone walks into Disney, it makes him or her feel happy, fun, or young again. What feeling are you trying to conjure up in your clients? Jot down on a piece of paper any adjectives that describe the feelings that your business should make your clients feel.

AESTHETICS

When it comes to branding, there is also a visual component; it must be aesthetically pleasing to prospective and current clients. The visual components of branding are items such as a logo, character or mascot, color schemes, and font styles. Visual branding can work one of two ways. First, you may build a relationship with a client, and when they see the visual representations of the company, it may reinforce the feeling they have about working with your business. Second, a prospective client may see the visual components of the company and either be intrigued enough by what they see to learn more, or get turned off by what they see and move on.

In a way, visual branding is similar to meeting someone for the first time. A person may be judged by the way they look, but once you get to know that person, what you see and what you feel may not match. In branding a company, however, it is important that you match the look of the business components with the way you want customers to feel about your company. For example, when you see a big, yellow, bouncing smiley face talking about rolling back prices, visions of Walmart® and its low-cost quality goods probably come to mind.

Think about and write down how your company logo, colors, font styles, and other representations should reflect the values, morals, strengths, and benefits of the coaching business. These representations should trigger a response from prospective and current clients when they see the representations so that they recognize your business and services instantly.

A small side note here. Branding at the level of a Walmart®, Target, Disney, or Coca-Cola® may or may not be in reach for your coaching business. The key element here is not to create a huge conglomerate in the coaching world, but rather to create a connection between your coaching business and the people, businesses, or organizations that can benefit from the services it provides.

After working through these three steps, you have to connect each element of the branding process to create a brand for you as the coach, for the coaching business, and for the services it provides. The company brand is the bridge between the company and its customers. It is possible to create a bridge that keeps attracting repeat business.

BRANDING IS PERCEPTION

Many companies create a brand based on how they want their customers to feel and connect with the company, products, and services. Unfortunately, it is not always about how a company wants their customers to feel. In reality, a brand is really about how current and potential customers perceive it to be. Finding the balance between how you want your brand to be perceived and how it is actually perceived is the key to successful branding.

For example, a nonprofit organization built a brand around helping battered women make it on their own by providing job training, business suits, and interview skills to help them land new jobs and start new lives. Potential donors of the organization, however, thought the organization existed to help an entirely different group of people. Because the perception was different from the reality, the non-profit continuously struggled with raising enough money to fund its programs and initiatives.

When brand perception is off-balance in a for-profit business situation, it can be even more important because it may mean the difference between running a profitable coaching company and having to close the business forever.

Three ways to balance the brand with audience perception:

1. Create and write a mission statement for the company that is understood and memorable.

2. Survey potential and current clients to see what they think the company does — what products and services it offers. If this matches the purpose of the company, then the brand and brand perception are in balance. If not, adjustments need to be made so that the balance is restored.

3. Segment messaging with the audience. No matter what type of coaching business you have, chances are you have several different market segments you cater to. When creating a brand and messaging, make sure this aligns with the audience you are targeting. For example, a wooden hangar manufacturer has two different audiences: high-end customers and budget-conscious customers. For this reason, it has two different webpages. One page speaks to and sells to

the high-end clientele while the other speaks to and sells to the budget-conscious clientele. It is all about how the copy is written, the price of the hangar, and how the hangar is branded to match the needs of the customer.

Customer perception is everything when it comes to branding. You can hire the most expensive branding company in the world to design your logo and create a brand for your business, but if the company brand and customer perception do not match, then it is all just a waste of time and money.

Creating a mission statement

One aspect of company branding is the company mission statement. Writing a mission statement mystifies most business owners, but a mission statement is not as baffling as some may think. When it comes down to the basic purpose of a mission statement, understanding its purpose makes writing it a simple, fast, and easy process. A mission statement is typically one or two sentences explaining why the company exists, the purpose of the company, and what the values of the company are. If you are drawing a blank in writing a mission statement, these three easy steps will help you break down the writer's block and write a compelling mission statement that does your coaching company justice.

- **Focus on purpose:** Many business owners tackling the task of writing a mission statement think the mission of the company has to be long, drawn out, and complicated. This is not true. You can and should be able to describe why your company exists and one of the key benefits clients derive from working with the company. Disney is one of the largest companies in the world, and its mission statement is summed up in four words: "to make people happy."

- **Focus on fulfillment:** Writing a mission statement and being able to fulfill it are two different things. Writing a mission statement is not about writing it for the sake of writing one. The company also has to have the ability to fulfill the mission statement, so be realistic about the mission statement as well. For example, an environmental organization may have a mission statement that says, "to make the world a safer place to live." This statement alone does not have much meaning attached to it because it is not clear as to how the company is going about making the world a "safer place to live." The Florida organization Save the Manatees focuses its world saving efforts to one area of the world, the water, and on one animal in the sea world, the manatees. Hence, the mission of Save the Manatee is, "Our mission is to protect endangered manatees and their aquatic habitat for future generations."

- **Write it down:** The first two steps were thought-provoking processes to encourage you to think about the purpose of your business and how you can go about fulfilling that purpose. Now it is time to put your mission statement into words and down on paper. Remember to keep the mission short, simple, and to the point. Your goal is to be able to hand the mission statement to complete strangers and have all of them understand what your company does.

Brand your business for modern times

Before the widespread use of Internet marketing, branding applied to tangible marketing collateral such as brochures, business cards, and letterhead. Modern times, however, have opened up the door to entirely new branding issues that directly relate to other marketing collateral such as websites, blogs, and social media networks. Modern times call for modern measures, so here are some branding exercises to walk through when evaluating the company brand online and offline.

Be search-engine friendly

Controlling the message current and potential customers see from your business is as important online as it is offline. Who does not sit down at their computer and use a search engine to find information out about companies, products, and services? When writing copy for the company website or posting blogs and articles online, make sure to include words in the copy that customers would use to find the services the coaching company provides. It is also important to control the name of the business by buying the domain name of the business and the top five variances. Variances may include buying the .com, .net, and .us versions of the domain name or other variances such as the business name spelled out completely, the business name acronym, and any other names your company goes by. If your coaching business does not include your name, for example, you may also wish to purchase your name as one of the domain names. When customers conduct an online search for your business name this helps to direct them to the coaching business website, even if in the end, all five or six domains point to the same website. You want to control the information someone sees when searching for your business, which is also being in control of the company branding.

Write and post with care

Publishing online is pretty easy to do. In some cases, it is too easy, which can cause a company branding problem. When you write and publish something online, it stays there forever, even if you delete it. Be careful what you say when you post something online. Make sure it reflects what the coaching business stands for and sheds a positive rather than a negative light on your business. Make a good first impression, and avoid racy or potential problematic photos or statements.

Match tangibles with intangibles

Branding requires consistency. This means the same colors, logo, look, and feel run through all of your marketing collateral — website, e-mails, online banner ads, print ads, letterhead, brochures, and business cards.

Personal and company image

In a coaching business, the coach's image and reputation can speak volumes to potential and current clients. If you miss appointments, deliver incomplete or work of poor quality, the client may leave with a bad impression of you and the coaching business. Not only does this affect the current client relationship, but it also puts the future relationship in jeopardy. Most individuals and corporate employees refer businesses that have done a good job for them, so make the right impression the first time. It can help you land one client and many more to come.

Image is much more than the way you handle clients. Reputation and professionalism both play an important role in image as well. Ethical behavior and trustworthiness are characteristics clients are willing to pay a higher fee to receive. Creating a good image and reputation is an ongoing process, but there are several things you can do to start off on the right foot.

A book is judged by its cover (and pages)

Creating a professional image is about what you look like on the outside and the professional way you come across to people when you meet them. Though you may be a genius in your field, if you show up at a client meeting in wrinkled clothes, with your hair standing up and coffee on your shirt, clients may be put off by your appearance. Being a professional starts from the outside and works its way in. Acting in a professional manner also adds to an image. Be aware of using foul language, allowing your bad habits to show, and other rude behaviors you may have. Work on correcting these habits and personality traits — even if it means creating a work persona that you put on when you talk to clients on the phone or walk into their office for a meeting.

What to do to create a professional image:

- Minimize any negative aspects that could be misconstrued as unprofessional, such as body language or appearance.

- Be honest with clients. Let them know what you can and cannot do, and be honest about their needs and your ability to fulfill them. This earns the client's respect.

- Dress professionally. Wear what you would expect the client to be wearing, or better. If you look sloppy, clients will believe your work is sloppy and may refrain from working with you.

- Under-promise and over-deliver. Do not make promises you cannot keep. Always clearly state what you can and cannot do. It is better to tell a client that something cannot be done and then end up pulling it off for them than telling them you can do something that you cannot deliver.

- Connect your personal image with the business image using marketing collateral such as business cards, letterheads, and report covers that represent you and the company.

Reputation

A reputation is even more important to potential and current clients than image because a bad reputation can damage an image. Several key areas affect the reputation of a coach. The primary element of a reputation is the work quality. Second in importance is the way the coach presents in public. Both of these elements help to build a positive and high-quality reputation rather than a negative and bad reputation. Remember, it is easier to maintain a good reputation than to have to overcome a bad reputation. Once you do something to hurt your reputation, it takes twice as much work to get back on track, and you may never fully recover. Therefore, it is imperative that you take steps necessary to maintain the best reputation possible.

One way to build a positive reputation quickly is to always perform your tasks and complete client interactions to the best of your ability. Because coaching in the industry or niche you are working in is your passion and area of expertise, this should not be hard to do. Make yourself readily available and easy to talk to, and keep the lines of communication open with your clients. Community involvement can also be a reputation-booster. Volunteering and working in the community allows you to shape a positive reputation while also doing good deeds. For example, if you are starting a tax coaching business, offer your services pro bono to non-profit organizations for a cause you support. Offer a free seminar to teach local businesses how to market their businesses on the Internet. Write and submit news pieces, editorials, or articles that offer a unique and interesting perspective to major newspapers and magazines within your field. For example, as a financial coach, offer a piece on debt management to a family magazine. Write a book on an aspect of your job and career. Getting your name out in the areas where your customers are is one of the best ways to build a high-quality reputation.

Weaving the brand together

Once you determine the look and feel you want to use to represent your personal and company brand, the most important aspect of branding is weaving it into every aspect of your coaching business. Branding encompasses everything that is internal and external with your company, so whether it is a memo that goes around to the internal employees of the coaching business or an e-mail that you are sending out to the client list, the brand standards apply. Some of the items you need to consider when applying the business brand include:

- Company logo
- Business cards
- E-mail signature
- Letterhead
- Brochures
- Marketing kit
- Website
- Blog
- Mailing envelopes
- Promotional items, such as pens, magnets, notepads, and drink cozies
- Proposals
- Client agreements or contracts

Marketing messaging

To start building a solid marketing foundation, one of the first tasks you will need to tackle is to determine your marketing message. A marketing message is the signal you want to send to your current and potential customers about your services. Some marketing professionals refer to this as a positioning statement because it is a written statement that "positions" your company and how you want it to come across to clients.

So, a positioning statement for a celebrity life coaching firm may be something like, "Zesty Life Coaches is a lifestyle resource offering practical resources and coaching programs to celebrities seeking to transform their life from less-than-optimal to exquisite. Unlike other lifestyle coaches, Zesty Life Coaches provides a step-by-step system and access to Zesty Living Designers that coach their clients through the process to achieve their unique, ultimate lifestyle."

After you get your positioning statement in order, then you want to establish one to three key messages you want to send to current and potential customers through your marketing efforts. These key marketing messages directly promote the products or services that you are touting for your business, but they are not taglines or memorable and catchy phrases. Instead, these are the messages that you want the audience to walk away with after reading your marketing collateral.

For example, Zesty Life Coaches may have these three key messages:

1. Zesty Life Coaches offers a proven system for creating exquisite lifestyles: The 7 Practices for Optimal Living.

2. Zesty Life Coaches provides useful resources and easy-to-implement tools to guide celebrities on their journey to living a Zesty Life.

3. Zesty Life Coaches offers coaching programs with Optimal Life Designers to help clients fast-forward their journey to living a Zesty Life.

To create your own key messages, list the three primary products or services you plan to offer your clients. Under each service list out how the service benefits clients. Now form messages with the services and the service benefit that you want clients to walk away with after exposure to your marketing initiatives.

Logos

Using a business logo is part of the branding strategy of the coaching business. Though a business logo is not as essential to a service-based business such as coaching as it is to a product business where product packaging is involved, many coaches opt to have a logo designed for their company.

You have several different avenues you can take in order to obtain a logo for your coaching business. First, you can hire a graphic designer to create a custom logo for your business. Generally, logo design of a custom logo starts at $200. There are also companies that sell ready-made logos, which you can purchase for as little as $25. These logos are not customized to your business and may be sold to many other companies to use, so it is a logo that is not exclusive to you. The benefits of buying a ready-made logo are that it is inexpensive and offers you an opportunity to create a brand for your business with the logo.

Finally, you can use software programs such as Microsoft Publisher or other desktop publishing programs to create your own logo. These programs typically have ready-made logos that you can use as is or personalize to fit your needs. If your design skills are up to par, you can also use these programs to create your own logo from scratch.

Business cards

Business cards are another marketing essential. You will need business cards for a variety of purposes that range from handing them out at a networking event to including one in a marketing kit you send to a prospective client.

As is the case with creating a logo, there are a variety of ways you can design and print business cards for your coaching business. The most expensive way to obtain business cards is to hire a graphic designer to design the business cards and then send the file off to a printer to have the cards printed. Websites such as Vistaprint (**www.vistaprint.com**) and 48hourprint.com (**www.48hourprint.com**) bring customized and professionally printed business cards down an expense level. These sites have professionally designed business card templates you can customize, personalize, and print at a reduced rate. You also have the option to upload your own design, so even if you have a graphic designer create the card, you can upload the card to one of these companies to professionally print the cards for less than most local printers will charge.

Desktop publishing programs also make business card templates available for you to create business cards. You can print these cards on your own printer using business card stock you can purchase at any major office supply or stationary store. Though this may be the least expensive way to get the business cards you need, it does require a time investment. Another disadvantage to creating and printing your own business cards is that it may cheapen the image of your company.

Website

Having a business website is an essential component of conducting business nowadays. Getting your business website up and running boils down to two main options. You can both build and maintain the website yourself or hire a professional to build and maintain it for you.

A myriad of options exist online for website companies that offer templates you can use to customize the look and feel of your business website. Other sites allow you to host your website with them and build your own website with a desktop publishing or design program such as Microsoft Publisher or Adobe® Dreamweaver. Taking this route may cost you anywhere from $4.95 per month to about $50 per month, depending on the website host you choose and the service options you choose to utilize through the host — such as memory storage amount, e-mail addresses, template options, and domain name.

The other main option is to hire a website designer to custom design a website for your business. The cost for a custom website design can run you anywhere from $100 for more of a basic website to thousands of dollars for a complex website. Not only do you need to consider the cost of hiring a designer to create your coaching business website, but most designers also charge you for making changes to the site after it is up and running.

If it is within your budget, choose a custom site for your initial design, although this will make any changes and maintenance that needs to be done difficult. Let the professionals do what they do best: build a great website. After the design of the website is settled, you also have to consider how you are going to obtain the content for the site. You either have to write the content on your own or hire a writer to create the content for you. This can be an added expense of anywhere from $100 to thousands of dollars, depending on how many webpages of content you need the writer to create for the site.

Brochures

Some coaches — the ones that meet more face-to-face with clients or the ones that send physical marketing packages to clients — find it helpful to have a company brochure. Brochures can be used in various marketing initiatives, from handing them out at tradeshows you may attend to including them in marketing kits to media professionals or potential clients. Coaches that focus more on online marketing typically replace a hard-copy brochure with an electronic format option. A third group of coaches uses a combination of an online and hard copy brochure.

As is the case with creating a logo, there are a variety of ways you can design and print brochures for your coaching business. The most expensive way to obtain brochures is to hire a graphic designer to design the business cards and then send the file off to a printer to have the brochures printed.

Vistaprint and 48hourprint.com also provide customizable brochure templates and printing options. These sites allow you to design your own brochure, add the content, and print the quantity you need at a reduced rate than most local printers. You can also opt to have the brochure designed by a professional or use desktop publishing software to create your own brochure layout and then upload the design to one of these websites to print the brochures.

Finally, you can buy brochure card stock that is scored for folding at your local office supply or stationary store. Use a desktop publishing program or templates to customize your brochures, and print them using your home computer and printer. Though this method can be highly cost-effective and you can print brochures as you need them rather than having to order hundreds or thousands at a time, it is important to make sure that the brochures do not lose the professional appearance you want them to have. If your brochure looks anything less than professional, it may turn clients away from working with you, which is the opposite effect a brochure should have.

Marketing kits

For service-based and high-ticket items such as coaching, you have to impress potential clients a bit more than a tangible product-based business in order to get them to buy. Putting together a marketing kit provides your coaching business with the opportunity to impress, motivate, and sell by providing your audience with more information than is possible to fit on a business card or in a brochure — or what you could say in an elevator pitch.

Marketing kits can be a powerful tool to convert sales; leave the kit as a takeaway from a client meeting, or drop it in the mail as a follow-up to a phone conversation or in response to an e-mail request from a prospect for more information. Always include two business cards and a company brochure, if you have one. A marketing kit is a comprehensive tool providing information to prospective clients that goes beyond handing them a business card and brochure alone. There are a few key essentials needed for your marketing kit:

- **Folder:** To build a marketing kit, you need a folder or some sort of holder for the marketing kit information. Keep in mind that the container the marketing kit comes in is the first impression your prospects receives, so you want it to look professional. You can accomplish this in one of two ways. First, you have the option of having folders professionally printed for less with online printers. A less expensive option is to have a label professionally printed that you can then affix to a linen pocket folder that can be purchased at any major office supply store.

- **Marketing template**: To weave the coaching company brand through all of the marketing pieces, you will next want to create a marketing template. A marketing template is the layout that each piece is printed on that is then included in the marketing kit.

- **USP**: Earlier in this book, you learned about creating a unique selling proposition to make your coaching business stand out from competitors. Make sure that your USP is included as part of the marketing kit information. Make sure you word it so that it shows how your company can benefit your customers from the customer's point of view.

- **Sell the benefits**: Most coaching businesses and businesses in general provide a list of features rather than the benefits a client enjoys by working with their company. When you list a coaching service in your marketing kit, make sure that you are listing out how this service benefits the client by revealing how it resolves an issue.

- **Service offering**: Include a bulleted list that allows the client to see your service offering at a quick glance. Follow the bulleted list with a more descriptive list of the coaching services offered by your company.

- **Testimonials:** Client testimonials can sell your services better than anything you can say to prospects. Include a full page of client testimonials, or have your clients record testimonials that you then include on a DVD or CD as part of the marketing kit.

- **Articles or media coverage**: Third-party endorsements from the media can also pack a powerful sales punch and should be included in the marketing kit. Include reprints of articles published about your company; DVDs of media interviews; or newspaper, magazine, or online article clips where you have been quoted as an expert source or your coaching business is mentioned.

Now that you have the foundational tools ready for marketing the coaching business, the next chapter covers how to attract clients to the coaching business.

CHECKLIST

✓ Create the company and your personal brand.

✓ Craft a unique selling proposition (USP).

✓ Use brand-building techniques online and offline.

✓ Create a positioning statement.

✓ Craft marketing messaging.

✓ Decide if a company logo is needed. If so, have one designed.

✓ Make a decision on how to create and print marketing items such as business cards, a website, brochures, and a marketing kit.

Chapter 10:
Finding Clients

In this chapter, you will:

- Create the marketing plan portion of the business plan.

- Learn ways to attract your target market with online marketing tactics.

- Discover offline methods for attracting the audience you are after.

The marketing plan is really the action part of your business; these are steps you can proactively take to promote the business, make people aware that the business exists, and find new clients. There are two sides to every marketing plan, which covers online and offline tactics you can use as a coach to attract the clients that fall into your target market and be hired by those clients. Ultimately, you can use the marketing plan as is to get started. The thing with marketing plans is that they are dynamic documents because after you implement the plan, you have to go back and evaluate the success or failure of your marketing tactics. Once you analyze the results, you can then tweak and adjust the marketing plan that needs to be implemented for the next six months to a year.

One important factor to keep in mind is that marketing a coaching business is a process. You cannot conduct a marketing activity one time and then decide that it is a complete failure because you do not see immediate results. You must take consistent action in implementing your marketing strategies for at least six months to a year.

The first part of the marketing plan is the marketing strategy. For a coaching business, three marketing strategies exist. Commit these three strategies to memory because every marketing activity covered in the remainder of the plan hinges on these three strategies:

1.   Gather qualified leads and followers to grow your subscriber list and database.

2.   Nurture the qualified leads and followers in your database by consistently getting in front of them, in various ways, with information about your coaching services.

3.   Convert the leads into clients and generate revenue by introducing them to your coaching services.

MARKETING FOUNDATION

Before you can start to implement and integrate the various marketing activities set forth in the marketing plan, you first have to build your marketing foundation. Building your marketing foundation includes putting together the marketing pieces and collateral, which was discussed in detail in Chapter 9. Because the first half of the marketing plan covers the online activities you can partake in to attract clients, the coaching business website needs to be up and fully functioning so you have a venue to drive traffic to when marketing your coaching services online.

To build the brand of the coaching business, which tackles the first marketing strategy, there are a few implementation strategies to include as part of the website to grab the attention of your ideal client. Traffic should be driven to the website from a variety of venues, which will be discussed later in the plan. Driving traffic to the home page of the website will be an important first step to gathering leads and converting them into clients. It will set the stage for learning more about these prospects and then up-selling them into the next logical service level you offer that fits their needs.

By incorporating certain elements into your website design, you can increase the credibility of your coaching website, allowing for the gathering of highly targeted leads that can be further qualified and turned into more revenue for the business. The following are elements your website should include:

Entice with an irresistible free offer

Offer an incentive to help capture information on the visitors to your website. An irresistible free offer may be a free downloadable report on a topic of interest to them. In exchange for the visitors to your site providing their name and e-mail address to you, provide something to them for free. Capturing these leads is the key to building your database of prospective clients. If visitors to your site are interested in accepting your free gift in exchange for providing you with their information, then they are potential clients for your business — at least up-front. The rest of your marketing activities help you to further qualify these leads and eventually move them into client status.

Further qualify subscribers

As part of the subscription process, add a one-question survey to the free offer subscription. Use a question that directly relates to the challenges your clients may face. For example, a private school coach that helps parents and clients maneuver the private school application, acceptance, and financial aid process may ask, "What is your biggest question about the private school admission process?" The point of the question is to find out what you prospects are thinking, feeling, or seeking information about. You can then use the information you gather to create solutions that cater directly to what clients and prospects are seeking.

Ensure comprehensive branding

Make sure that your branding is carried throughout all of your website pages, auto-responders, and other marketing collateral for consistency purposes. Use the same color schemes, font styles, layouts, and templates throughout all of your materials.

Optimize your pages

Use keywords in the copy of your website that prospective clients would use to search for the products or services your coaching business offers; this is the basis of search engine optimization (SEO). Choose one or two keywords to focus on for each page of your site, and then scatter the keywords, phrase, and combinations of the phrase in the beginning, in the middle, and toward the end of your copy. Make sure that the copy is written to include the keywords so that text flows and sounds natural. You can use free keyword tools such as the Google AdWords™ keyword tool, or you can hire a professional keyword or SEO professional to help you come up with a list of keywords to include on the site.

If you provide services to a confined geographic area, be sure to include keywords that speak about the area you cover. You should also use the keywords in the page titles, headlines, and sub-headlines in the copy on each page.

INTERNET MARKETING AND LIST-BUILDING

A growing business requires you to steadily grow your existing database by gathering highly targeted new leads. This creates the foundation for significant business growth and increased revenue for your coaching business. Once you fill your database with the ideal prospects you seek, you can then work on selling them your fee-based products and services by communicating with them on a regular basis. Here are some ways to keep your clients up to date:

E-newsletter

Regularly publish an e-mail newsletter to create an automatic lead-capturing system online and as a communication tool for your existing database.

Editorial calendar

Create an editorial calendar to map out discussion topics for the next six weeks or so. Block out time on your calendar each week to create this content and post it on your blog. You can also use existing content you have — such as products, presentations, and reports — to break down and turn into blog posts. Each blog post should be approximately 200–400 words. The editorial calendar can also be used for creating e-newsletter articles and social media updates.

SOCIAL MEDIA

Harnessing the power of social media outlets drives more targeted traffic to your website, which in turn will drive more clients to your coaching business. This provides you with the opportunity to communicate with your target market on a more regular basis and in different ways, and it can have a powerful and positive effect on growing your list and your coaching business. Social media networks include Facebook, Twitter, LinkedIn, and YouTube. Each social media network works slightly different, so you will need to familiarize yourself with each one. The following sections, however, go into detail on how you can utilize each network as part of your social media marketing efforts. You can implement the following social media strategies:

Facebook "Like" page

Recently, the Facebook Fan page was changed to "Like" page; where users can click a "like" button that makes them a member of a certain page. The only difference in the two is the wording — once you "like" a particular page, you become a fan.

Create a Facebook "Like" page that speaks directly to your target markets and focuses on the geographic area of your business (if applicable). To build your fan base, include a special announcement in your e-newsletter to drive traffic to the Facebook page. Be sure to include a link to your business Facebook page in every piece of correspondence you have with your prospects and client. This way, you are creating a two-way street: driving traffic from social media to your website and vice versa. If you can gather video or audio testimonials from clients, these are also great ways to let your services speak for themselves. If not, then record case studies or scenarios where you can illustrate how your service helped a client to gain success.

You can use the Facebook "Like" page in various ways, including sharing your blog posts with links to drive them directly to where the post sits on your site; posing questions to your audience in an effort to engage them and make it more of an interactive experience. This also allows you to evaluate who your audience is on your "Like" page so you can then work on funneling them into the appropriate service level of your business. You can also integrate your Twitter™ account with your "Like" page so your updates get more exposure and even add to the sidebar information about your business.

Facebook profile

Because Facebook limits actual profiles to individuals, it is better practice to create a Facebook "Like" page for your coaching business and integrate your personal Facebook page with your business's page. Use your personal profile page to talk about your professional relation to the business, join relevant groups, and RSVP to events that connect to your target market. Join groups or become a fan of any professional organizations you belong to and any of your competitors. Also, integrate your Twitter account with your profile so your updates get more exposure.

Twitter

Twitter is another social media marketing tool you can use to promote your coaching business online. Use Twitter to share information, products, and services related to your business. This helps to position you as an expert resource for information without always trying to sell them on your products and services. Aim for 80 percent information sharing and 20 percent promotion. You can integrate your tweets with your blog posts and articles, which is a highly effective way to attract followers, and it permits you to communicate with your followers and drive them to your website. Almost all tweets should include a link to a specific blog article, product, or service on your website. Sharing helpful tips or information on Twitter has to be done within the 140 characters that Twitter allows for tweets. Make your tweets intriguing, and then send your followers somewhere they can get more information by including a link. Twitter allows you to share information, but your goal is to use it as a tool to drive traffic to your coaching website — as is the goal with all of your social media marketing. Be sure to use the "shorten URL" feature on Twitter to keep the length of the URLs as short as possible; bit.ly (**www.bit.ly**) is a URL shortener that also tracks your links, giving you information on how active a certain post is.

Follow people you admire — such as authors, bloggers, e-zines you read, seminars you attend, or leaders in your field — as well as your competitors. Visit these profiles and their lists of followers to find people to follow that fit your target market. Consider having a custom background created that matches your brand in addition to the sidebar information about your business. A dramatic or attractive background can boost interest for followers.

LinkedIn®

LinkedIn is another online source for professionals, business owners, and entrepreneurs that can develop your coaching services. Add a direct link to your website's home page in your profile so people can take advantage of your free offer right away. Your LinkedIn profile should connect to your blog for further exposure of your content. You can start connecting with individuals that are in related businesses. This is a great way to connect with possible joint venture partners, potential clients, and other referral sources. Also look for people located in the geographic area your business covers, if applicable. This is a great way to connect with potential clients as well as referral sources.

LinkedIn provides a built-in application for gathering recommendations from clients you have worked with or other professionals on LinkedIn that you have done business with. Spend some time once per quarter gathering recommendations from your contacts. LinkedIn can be a very powerful tool, especially after you have connected with at least 500 other professionals. Even if you cannot get recommendations, you need to use LinkedIn as a tool to connect with your target audiences.

YouTube®

Create and use a free YouTube account to upload instructional videos that speak on a certain point of interest to your target audiences. You can also turn each of your written blog posts and/or e-newsletter articles into a video. You are providing just enough information to encourage your audience to gain more information by going to your website. These videos can also be added to your Facebook profile and fan page for additional exposure.

Remember, you want to be everywhere that your target audience is, and these are the social media websites your target market is using.

Blog

Having an up-to-date blog is one of the primary ways people are going to find your coaching business online because search engines look for updated content when determining page rank. Share your expertise about your business, industry, or niche in your blog posts. Then, integrate your blog with the social media sites (Facebook, LinkedIn, and Twitter) to help drive traffic to your site. Mix it up between longer, more word-driven posts talking about industry specific news and shorter posts about a new product or service. Any videos or images you can add will also help make your blog more three-dimensional. Just remember: Your blog should not be just about your business; you want to connect with your clients, not hard sell them your services. You can use complimentary blogging platforms such as Wordpress (**www.wordpress.com**) or Blogger (**www.blogger.com**) to create and maintain a blog.

For a blog to be an effective marketing tool, it is imperative for you to post on your blog at least two to three times a week. Blog posts should include keywords your potential clients and target markets use to find information on the services you provide.

You can also map out a year's worth of e-newsletter content, tweets, and public relations campaigns that are all built around the same editorial content topics to keep everything streamlined and in alignment.

Article marketing

Use content you have created and develop it into new articles — aim for at least one article per week. Popular topics for coaches include how-to articles and articles that cover specific steps or detailed information on topics relevant to your audience. For example, a business coach may write an article on the top five ways to make sure that your business succeeds its first year in existence. A marketing coach may write an article on the top seven ways to drive targeted traffic to a business website.

You can use these articles to disseminate information via your e-newsletter, upload them to article directories, such as EzineArticles (**www.ezinearticles.com**) and Amazines (**www.amazines.com**), use them on your blog, and post them on your social media networks. Make sure your articles are also rich with keywords. Article marketing is one of the most effective and least expensive ways to drive targeted traffic to your coaching website. Your goal in using article marketing is to drive visitors to the appropriate page of your site — where your free offer sits. Your goal is to get them to request the free offer in exchange for gathering their information. You do this by including a strong call to action in the resource box of each article you submit online. This is also a lead-in for other marketing communication efforts and up selling to your paid services.

You can also record the articles you write and repurpose them into videos and podcasts. Upload the podcasts to your blog and create an audio or video series that you can include on your blog, distribute in your e-newsletter, upload to YouTube, or send out as a special series of e-mail blasts to your subscriber list. Podcasts can also be uploaded and distributed on iTunes.

Link building

On a weekly basis, visit the business websites, blogs, and forums that are related to your business, niche, or industry. These are additional places where your audience is looking for information and another place where you can find information, as well as start building relationships with other coaching companies. Post a relevant, valuable comment on at least five sites per week. Forums and blog posts allow you to post your name, business name, and a link back to your website — again, driving traffic back to your website. This is an indirect way of promoting your business by positioning yourself as an expert and a resource while creating additional exposure for your business. You want your name, company name, and website address all over the sites that have anything to do with your business. If your potential clients are visiting these sites, you want them to see you there too.

Sites of this nature may also offer an opportunity for you to become a guest author or article contributor, which allows you to use content you have to share your expertise with a new audience, gain the attention of your target market by positioning yourself as the expert you are, and broaden your reach.

Direct response

You also need to focus on nurturing the existing leads you have and the new ones you are gathering by consistently communicating with your database. You can communicate with your database by sending out auto-responders and promotional e-mails at least once or twice a month. Promotional e-mails may include a special offer on one of your coaching services, announce the dates of an upcoming teleseminar, or incorporate a case study that illustrates a problem one of your clients faced and how your services resolved the problem. Promotions and case studies can also be included in the e-newsletter.

TRADITIONAL MARKETING IS NOT DEAD

Now that you have a variety of ways you can market your coaching business online, it is time to take a look at the avenues available for marketing your business offline.

List building

Though there are numerous ways you can build your list using online marketing tactics, there are just as many ways you can build your list with offline marketing tactics. In fact, the best way to build your list is to combine your online and offline list building efforts. Some of the ways you can build your list offline include:

- Be a guest or participate in as many teleseminars as possible.

- Be a regular guest on various Internet radio shows.

- Advertise with organizations and associations that are targeting your ideal clients.

- Interview well-known people in your niche and post these interviews online and in print publications.

- Submit articles to print publications read by your target market.

- Advertise in print publications your target market reads.

- Add your free irresistible offer to the back of your business card.

- Do a postcard mailing to a high-quality mailing list.

- Attend live networking events and seminars that cater to your target market.

- Periodically ask past and current clients for referrals.

- Public relations program.

One of the key programs that will help to boost your business and subscriber list while increasing credibility is publicity. Publicity is a low-cost, effective way to reach your target audience. The purpose of publicity for a coaching business is:

- To inform potential clients and referral sources about you, your company, your services, and how you can help them.

- To educate the media and potential clients to shape attitudes and behaviors and change perceptions about the coaching industry.

- To effectively communicate your marketing messages.

Public relations (PR) is one of the easiest, most cost-effective ways to promote who you are and what you do so you can get more clients and more sales for your business. PR builds credibility and visibility that helps you gain new clients and can increase your income. Public relations is the art of building favorable and profitable interest in you, your business, or your service by creating a "buzz" in the marketplace. PR gets your message across and tells others about you, what you do, and why it is important to them. Public relations lends credibility to you and builds your reputation from a third-party point of view; therefore, it is often more valuable than advertising alone. PR is effective because it:

- Creates awareness of your brand.

- Communicates the benefits of your products and services.

- Positions you as an expert.

- Generates sales and leads.

PR is usually free and lends more credibility to your claims than paid advertisements. It is the most cost-effective way to generate interest about your coaching business and reach existing and potential clients. When people read about you in the media from a journalist or hear about you on the radio, you get instant third-party validation and receive positioning as an expert in your field. Although a paid advertisement placed in a publication can cost you tens of thousands of dollars each time it is run, a well-placed article is much more cost effective and adds value to your business.

Trade publications have a number of subscribers, and most have thousands of readers, each of who is a prospect that may need the services your coaching business offers. At the very least, the readers likely know someone who needs the services you provide. In addition, this positions you as an expert, which produces a premium price for your services because people are more willing to pay more for your expertise. This often removes price as an obstacle to overcome in the process of attracting new clients. PR also levels the playing field and allows small businesses to appear larger than they are and compete on the same level as larger businesses.

PR helps you attract qualified prospects and leads. The more people know about you, the higher the level of trust it builds, which makes it more likely they will contact you and refer others to you. As an added bonus, current clients get the confirmation they need that your business is the best one to do business with. Here is how to get started:

Develop a media list

A media list should include local and national outlets that will have an interest in covering your story. It is important to find individual reporters, journalists, and writers for the publication that would have an interest in covering your story. You will need to gather and maintain a PR contact list for these local journalists and publications, either by paying for these subscriptions or doing independent research online.

Implement editorial calendars

Most print publications publish a calendar outlining topics they will be covering throughout the year, called an editorial calendar. Use the editorial calendars of your top media outlets to help you to develop story ideas for promoting your business. These lists are useful when pitching story ideas, so you can tie in your story with these topics. Also monitor and identify publicity opportunities from journalists and lists such as Help a Reporter Out (**www.helpareporter.com**) and Pitch Rate (www.pitchrate.com). By responding to a reporter's source query, you are establishing yourself as an expert in your coaching niche. Your credibility and reputation can only build if you are positively quoted in a news article.

Write a pitch

Your pitch should be personalized to the person you are pitching the story to. Mention similar stories they have covered, or point out why their readers would be interested in the story you have to tell. The pitch should also include an overview of the story and have the press release attached for more details.

To start, determine the top three local media outlets for newspaper, TV, and radio in the area where you run your coaching business. Send press releases to specific journalists or editors, and follow up accordingly.

Write a monthly press release

You should send out one press release per month for special events, workshops, or webinars you are promoting. An easy strategy if you do not have something specific to promote for the month is to use your blog or monthly e-newsletter articles as a press release. This way, you leverage your writing and are able to use your content in multiple places and for multiple purposes.

When writing a press release for online media, the main goal is to get keywords picked up by search engines. A search engine optimized (SEO) press release is geared toward specific keywords rather than a specific story idea. SEO press releases are written and used online in order to increase the amount of traffic you drive to your website. Keyword-focused press releases are generally distributed through wire services. Many companies — especially larger ones — are sending press releases through these online services for the primary purpose of driving traffic to their websites. Submit your monthly press releases to the top five online press release distribution sites, which include one paid service and four free services.

ONLINE PRESS RELEASE DISTRIBUTION CHANNELS	
PRWeb.com	$80/release
I-newswire.com	Free
IdeaMarketers.com	Free
Free-press-release.com	Free
24-7pressrelease.com	Free

Pitch to the media and follow up frequently

Once a month when you write the press release, pitch the story to the appropriate media outlets. Follow up with each media contact you have pitched the story to, and make sure they received the information. Use the follow-up as an opportunity to see if they are interested in covering the story.

Speaking opportunities

Speaking opportunities can be an excellent source for new prospects and sale conversions for a coach. You can use speaking opportunities to expand your reach and position yourself as an expert in your field. Offsite speaking engagements help you reach potential clients while simultaneously enforcing the establishment of your expertise. Some options include being a guest speaker for radio shows, webinars, and workshops — online or live.

Speaking engagements allow coaches to connect face-to-face with current and potential clients and referral sources. It provides the opportunity to showcase areas of expertise, schedule appointments with potential clients, and even close sales.

Have a system in place to gather the names and contact information of the attendees of the show or event where you are speaking. Run a contest to gather attendee names, e-mail addresses, and telephone numbers; this allows you to build your list of leads and provides you with the opportunity to follow up with those leads to try to convert them into clients.

Speaking engagements are also prime locations for selling services on the spot. Run a show or speaking engagement special so if a prospect becomes a client at the show, they receive a special discount or bonus offer.

Write a book

The purpose of writing a book is to promote your expertise. You can write and self-publish a book using a print-on-demand website online (such as **www.lulu.com** or **www.cafepress.com**) on a topic that is hot in your industry. You can sell the book on coaching websites and at public speaking engagements. Book sales are another lead-gathering tactic, where you can then communicate with book buyers to convert them into a coaching client.

CHECKLIST

- ✓ Implement the marketing plan portion of the coaching business plan.

- ✓ Attract your target market by consistently implementing online marketing tactics.

- ✓ Attract members of your target audience by simultaneously implementing offline methods in conjunction with your online marketing tactics.

Chapter 11:
Client Interaction

In this chapter, you will:

- Learn about the various touch points you will have with clients.

- Discover effective ways to interact with the client from the point they contract your coaching services and throughout the relationship.

- Uncover post-relationship communications to help elicit repeat and referral business from the client.

- Find out some of the specific ways to tell clients that what they have been doing is not positively impacting their personal or professional life, or business and encourage them to implement necessary changes.

Though all of your marketing efforts are touch points with your prospects, once you sign an agreement with the prospect, from that point on you are interacting with a client. Landing a new client is one vital side of your coaching business, but working with the client in a professional manner to keep the client is the other integral part of running a successful coaching business.

A solid foundation of success for any coach is having a high-quality level of communication with the client from the very beginning. Communication includes both the verbal and written communication you will have with a client as a coach. If you start off with open lines and effective forms of communication with the client, it will make working with the client a much easier and smoother process. Effective communication is the key to any solid business relationship, so it is imperative that you learn how to communicate and interact with clients at the various touch points that take place before, during, and after the relationship begins.

Luckily, effective communication is something that you can learn. Practice makes perfect with acquiring and refining your communication skills, so if you do not possess the essence of communication naturally, make a concerted effort to get your communication skills up to par.

WRITTEN COMMUNICATION (BEFORE THE RELATIONSHIP)

Written communication is just as important as verbal communication, and putting items in writing can even help to clarify and solidify the information, so as to avoid problems and misunderstandings later.

Once the client wants to pursue working with you, your next step is to provide a written contract or agreement to the client that spells out the details of your working relationship. As you will quickly see, a contract is a must-have for any coach working in virtually any field because putting the agreement in writing details precisely what your role is in the transaction, what the client's role is, the payment structure, and other terms and conditions that must be met.

A contract includes every important detail, including what the relationship entails, all the specifications, the timeline, and the payment details. Another important aspect of the contract is a termination clause, which provides a way for either party in the transaction a way to end or terminate the agreement. For example, if the client is not happy with the quality of the work, a termination clause spells out the specific steps the client has to take to end the agreement. The same holds true for the coach.

As you work with the client, if situations change then the contract or client agreement also needs to be changed. You and the client need to have a conversation about what the changes are, and an addendum to the contract needs to be created and agreed to by both parties. For example, if additional work time is required or the client wishes to focus on a goal that falls out of the scope of the original goal, outline the changes in the addendum to the contract. Always put changes in writing, and have your client agree to the changes before proceeding.

Contracts are legally binding, which is why it is important that everything is in writing and that there is a signature from you and the client on the contract. After the contract is in place and you start to work with the client, both verbal and written communications are involved in taking the relationship from the contract stage to completion.

SIX ESSENTIAL METHODS OF COMMUNICATION

Aspects of communication are numerous, and all forms of communication cannot be exhausted in this book. However, there are six areas of communication specific to coaches that are necessary for you to take heed. Communication is similar to a well-oiled machine, so while each part of communication is separate, in totality, the communication efforts must work together in order for the overall relationship to function properly.

Utilizing these six methods of communication will help you to solidify the successful completion of each client project.

Tip 1: Carefully choose your words

Most of the time, it is not what you have to say to a client that is the important part, but rather how you say it to the client. Think about what you are going to say before you speak. Once you know what you need to say, make sure that you word it in a way that does not sound negative, combative, or give off the wrong impression to the client. For example, rather than say, "You are doing it wrong," say something less abrasive, such as, "Have you ever approached it like this...?"

Do you see the difference? You are saying the same thing, essentially, without attacking the client — or at least from making the client feel as if you are attacking them.

Tip 2: Ask questions first

Gathering information from the client at the beginning of the project sets the stage for the rest of the project. If you jump right in offering the client suggestions without first asking all of the right questions, then you may end up embarrassed. Never make assumptions about clients or what they have tried before hiring you as a coach. Instead, ask questions of the client to garner the information you need. Gather all of the facts and lay them out in front of you before you assume what the client expects out of the project.

When you ask questions, really listen to the client's responses. Clients provide you with many clues with what they say, so rather than formulating what you are going to say in your head while the client is talking, make sure that you fully understand what the client is saying. Repeat back to them what you interpret to make sure that you understand correctly.

Most clients are more than willing to answer your questions, but some are more resistant than others. If clients resist fully answering your questions, simply explain that there are several different ways to accomplish their goal, and your questions are simply for clarification purposes to make sure that you implement the most effective strategy.

Tip 3: Be enthusiastic

To each client that hires you, his or her goal is the most important one of all your clients. This means that even if this is the 100th time you have worked on a similar goal, you have to be enthusiastic about tackling their goal. Although there are times that you will simply sit and listen to what the client is saying, your body language, responses, and facial expressions have to portray excitement rather than disinterest and boredom. Keep eye contact with the client, smile, and show your interest in what the client is saying every time you meet or talk with him or her.

Tip 4: Keep it simple

Coaches tend to use jargon and lingo that pertains to their specialty but means nothing to the client they are speaking to. When you talk to your clients, you need to address them in a style and manner that makes sense to them. You will also run into clients that like to receive different information in different ways, so you are going to have to read the client so that you are responding to their needs. For example, some clients want to know all of the details no matter how small. Other clients only want you to tell them what they absolutely need to know and nothing more. Try to disseminate information in small chunks so it is easier for the client to take in and process.

Tip 5: Be a good listener

A popular saying is that humans have two ears and one mouth for a reason — to listen. Whether this is true or not, when you are working as a coach, it is paramount that you listen to precisely what your client is saying. You can only accomplish the goal and fill your client's needs if you know what those needs are. Be an active participant in a conversation with the client, so say what you need to say and share with him or her, but also actively listen to what he or she is saying to you as well.

Tip 6: Get to know your client

Find the right balance between getting to know your client professionally and getting to know the client on a personal level. Getting to know your client better can help make you communicate better with them. For example, if in a discussion you find out that the client is more of a morning person, you may want to schedule your meetings and phone calls with the client during his or her peak performance times. If you learn that the client has children who play sports, you may want to occasionally ask how they are playing. It is important not to go overboard, but mixing some personal and professional time can deepen your relationship with clients.

CASE STUDY: COACHING
CLIENTS

Peg Rowe
Peg Rowe Associates
1448 Lawrence Ave
Lake Forest, IL 60045
(847) 234-3754
peg@pegroweassociates.com

Peg Rowe has been a coach since 2001, and has a BS and MS, as well as completed the coaching training program at the Coaches Training Institute (CTI), the Gestalt Coaching Program at the Gestalt Institute of Cleveland, and the Organizational and Relationship System Coaching Program through the Center for Right Relationship and CTI.

Her business is comprised of coaching, facilitating, and consulting. Typically, she works with 12 to 15 coaching clients at a time, in addition to working with three to five teams. Her clients are from referrals, as most coaching clientele. They are usually current and past clients, as well as colleagues. She focuses on Executive and Leadership coaching, working with senior leaders of organizations. "My clients are typically working at Fortune 500 companies, as well as occasionally entrepreneurs and leaders of not-for-profits," she said.

Because many of her clients work in large corporations, she does a combination of in-person and phone coaching. She also works with teams in yearlong programs that focus on enhancing team effectiveness and producing results. "My clients are usually high potential leaders engaging a coach to enhance their performance as a leader. This work is transformational, engages individuals at a deep level, and some would consider the impact spiritual," she said.

Because many of her clients work in large corporations, she does a combination of in person and phone coaching. She also works with teams in yearlong programs that focus on enhancing team effectiveness and producing results.

"My clients are usually high potential leaders engaging a coach to enhance their performance as a leader. This work is transformational, engages individuals at a deep level, and some would consider the impact spiritual," she said.

All of her clients are unique, which allots her the opportunity to interact different types of people and situations. Rowe remembers coaching a woman who was an executive in a male-dominated corporation and industry. "She had been successful in field roles and was recently promoted to corporate as a member of the senior leadership team. As the newest member of the team, she had taken a low-key role. Her boss, the division president, saw her potential and specifically wanted her to step up to a more visible presence," said Rowe.

The two worked on dismantling limiting paradigms and shifting to powerful new beliefs, creating strategies for bringing her voice to discussions and decisions. Rowe said, specifically, they focused on taking a leadership role in team meetings and bringing clarity to her vision of success. As a result, the woman's role expanded twice and she was recognized for her contemporary leadership style. "During the succession planning process, she was identified as a key player and is being groomed to replace her boss. She is self-assured, leading with confidence and ease," said Rowe.

THE RIGHT WAY TO ASK QUESTIONS

Rather than sounding like a drill sergeant, blurting out questions to a client machine-gun style, there is a fine art to asking questions in a way that does not make you seem overbearing. You have to be able to ask clients questions to uncover the details. Questions can also help to clarify information you already have to ensure that you understand them and their needs. Nothing wastes more time than working with a client to later find out that you approached it in an incorrect manner because you did not understand all of the facts. It is not just a waste of your time when this happens, but it may also cause you to lose the client. Here are some tips and approaches you can take when it is time to weave some questions into your client interaction.

1. Set a goal with your question

It may seem like a leap at first, but one of the first questions you should ask a client is what his or her expectations are. What results are they trying to achieve? This is a goal-setting question, so once you know what your goal is, it is much easier to fill in the steps required to get your client from where they are today to where they need to be as the coaching relationship comes to an end. In reality, you should know the answer to this question before you even start working with a client. Typically, this is a question that happens at the courting stage of the relationship, but it is also a good idea to clarify that the goal is the same when you start to work together. Your belief of what the goal is and the client's belief of what the goal is must be the same or the results may be way off course.

2. Lead into a question

Preface your questions by first sharing information with the client. Position yourself as the expert you are by sharing knowledge and experience about the question you are about to ask. Then pose the question at the end. For example, you may use the lead-in, "Did you know that…" Sharing some information with the client up-front sets the stage for the question you need the client to answer.

3. Repeat for comprehension

Once a client answers the question, reform the follow-up question so it repeats the client's responses to make sure that you comprehend what the client is saying. For example, if the client tells you three different goals they want to accomplish then you may ask, "Can I go over the goals with you again to make sure that I understand?" Then go through the goals one at a time and how you interpreted what the client said to make sure you are both on the same page.

4. Get the client to make a decision

Throughout the process of working with a client, you are going to come to points where the client needs to make a decision. Even once the client tells you which choice they make, you may want to make sure that this is the path they are committed to. You can phrase the question to be something like, "Are you committed to…" or simply restate the answer for clarification purposes. It is not about repeating exactly what the client says to you back to them like you are a parrot. It is more about allowing the client to hear what they are saying to make sure that what they are saying and what they mean is the same thing.

5. Mix up open- and closed-ended questions

Find the right balance of closed- and open-ended questions to ask the client. Yes and no questions only get so much information out of a client. Too many open-ended questions, however, can make the client feel like they are doing all of the talking. Both types of questions call help you gather the information you need, so use both versions of questions to attain the information you need. Yes and no answers only work for confirmation, whereas open-ended questions encourage them to share details, providing you with the information you need to make key decisions.

6. Leverage answers for new questions

Use the answers a client provides to a question to formulate another question. This methodology works best for clarification questions, especially if the client gives you an answer you were not prepared to receive.

Using the response to ask the next question helps you to uncover the true meaning behind the response and to make sure you understand what the client is saying.

7. Approach from a different angle

If you ask a question, but the client does not provide you with an appropriate response, then you may have to ask the question again from a different angle. Rather than saying you do not understand the client's response, simply compose the question in a different way to try to get the answer you need.

8. Get down to the nitty-gritty

Clients may glaze over a question you ask or give you such a broad response that it is not enough information for you to go on. Be straightforward with the client and really dig deep to get to the details. For example, if the client gives you a broad response as a goal, then ask a question to start narrowing down the focus of the goal. You may even want to ask the client, "What do you see as our first step?"

9. Be prepared

Each meeting or discussion you have with a client should have a specific purpose. You should always conduct your own research and go to the meeting prepared to accomplish the goal set for the meeting. For example, if you are helping the client to develop a list of education courses to advance in their career, then you should spend time on education sites for the industry in which the client is involved. You will have an idea of which courses or classes the client needs to take and a list of questions to ask the client to make sure you guide the client in the right direction.

LISTENING IS JUST AS IMPORTANT AS TALKING

What you say is as important as the information you take in from the client. As much as you can work toward refining your communication skills, there are also steps you can take to improve your listening skills.

Be an active listener

To be active, you need to participate in the conversation, so while talking may not be necessary, you need to react to what the client is saying. Keep eye contact, shake your head, smile, or show an expression of surprise. Whatever is an appropriate reaction, make sure that you are fully engaged in the conversation when you are the listener.

Stay focused

It happens. People start blabbing on and on about a topic, and your thoughts start to wander. When you are listening to what a client is saying, you have to stay focused on the client rather than think about what you are going to have for lunch or the host of other tasks you could be tackling right now rather than listen to this client go on and on. When your thoughts are not on the conversation at hand, you are not focused, so clear your mind of everything except what the client is saying.

Take notes

Jot down notes or ask the client's permission to record your discussions. It is impossible to remember everything a client says, even if you are intently listening. Taking notes makes you a better listener because it forces you to process what you are hearing to get it down on paper. Taking notes creates reference material that you can refer to later and throughout working with the client.

Ask more questions

Responding to what a client says by asking a question illustrates that you are listening and even makes you a better listener because you are waiting for the response to your question. Asking questions and listening go hand in hand. The process is a give-and-take situation between you and the client. By listening and asking questions yourself, you can be sure both of you are on the same page.

EFFECTIVE REPORT WRITING

IMPORTANT NOTE: Keep in mind that some clients would rather you not discuss sessions with others. This is where confidentiality should be considered before proceeding to construct a progress report for your client. Many coaches do not write progress reports unless it is a special case and you have the complete discretion of the client. Make sure that you have the client's full permission before proceeding into this section.

If you are working with a business client, you may also be required to provide written reports to update the client on the status of the coaching sessions with individuals or groups of the employees. Though you may have a discussion before or after (or both) you send a written report to a client, it is important that reports are detailed enough to provide information such as what stage the coaching relationship currently is, as well as any setbacks, changes, or progress made. Reports should provide a high level of detail to make sure that the client has all of the information necessary and to prevent misunderstandings that can occur.

Clients may request weekly or monthly updates or as certain milestones are met. You may want to spell out report submission terms in your contract. Other times, coaches simply provide reports to clients on a regular basis or only upon request from the client.

Nine times out of ten, your coach reports and updates will be sent via e-mail. In fact, even if you provide a client with a verbal report, you should send the written report as a follow-up to your conversation. For example, your client calls you on your cell phone to get an update of what is happening with the group of managers you are working with in a company. You can provide the client with an update on each manager, but when you return to the office, send the client an e-mail that starts off with something to the effect of, "Per our conversation earlier today…" and then outline the details of the update you provided. Written reports make communication clear and precise, so it is worth investing the time it takes to write them.

The key element a written report must possess is organization. A clearly organized report encourages the client to read it, while a disorganized and complex report can discourage a client from reading it. Write a concise, detailed, and effective report to help ensure the client reads it and receives the essential information the report contains.

When it comes to writing these reports, there are various aspects to take into consideration. In fact, as a coach, you will use these reports as a way of communicating as well as relaying your needs. Therefore, you need to write reports correctly to communicate with your client.

Writing progress reports

Think back to your school days. When teachers sent home progress reports each quarter or semester, the report provided your parents with an update on where you stood with grades, assignments, and behavior before report card time. The report either gave you a green light to keep doing things the same or a warning that it was time to make some changes before report cards came out. Progress reports do something similar for clients in that they give the client a status report and provide the client with the ability to ask you to make changes, as needed, to achieve the goals of the project.

The length and style of coach progress reports are not set in stone, so the report can be tailored to fit the needs of your business or the needs of the client. If a one-page report provides all of the details, then use a one-page report.

Always be up-front and honest in your reports. If there is a problem, you want to bring it to the client's attention sooner rather than later. You can put the client relationship in jeopardy if you try to hide things or gloss over things in your report. You can and should include pertinent information in the report. Here are some ideas on specific areas that are typically covered in a coaching progress report as it relates to the progress status.

Overall summary

Start out with an overall status summary. You can spell out the accomplishments to date and let the client know the current status.

Outline of accomplishments

Because the summary is a brief overview of the accomplishments, the next section of the report goes into detailed accomplishments. Provide as much detail as possible without being redundant. Provide the client with information on what has progressed since the previous progress report.

Completion status

Next, provide a client with a list of the completed tasks. Include the task description, date of completion, and what percentage of the overall relationship or goal accomplishments is complete.

Outline tasks to be completed

Then, outline the tasks that are pending, in order, so the client sees a picture of what is left to be done.

Issues or concerns

If you encountered problems let the client know what the problems were and how you did or did not overcome, which provides the client with an opportunity to examine the problem and help you find a resolution. This is a great area to list the challenges you have faced and how you have overcome them and also to ask for assistance.

Set expectations with your clients on progress reports at the beginning of your relationship. You may also want to spell out the report schedule in the contract or in writing for the client. Reports may be something clients want and expect, or it could be something they are not interested in receiving. Plus, if you outline the timeframe between progress reports — for example, once a week — the client knows when to expect the next report.

Writing final reports

Although progress reports keep clients abreast of the situation along the way, the final report is the one provided to the client when the relationship comes to a conclusion. A final report signals the end of one goal, but it may be the starting point for a new goal.

The final report is similar to a progress report, only without looking ahead. It should also include a few other details and informed opinions you may have regarding the goal completion or achievement. These reports can be an outstanding way to convey your message to the client about future goals. Sell yourself here, letting them know what you believe is the next step. A final report includes:

Summary

A summary is the best place to start and provides the same information the summary does in a progress report. Outline the overall accomplishments you made while working with the client and the goals that were not achieved. The summary is a brief overview of what you will go into detail about later in the report.

Outline

Outline the overall scope of the relationship and what the original goals were. You can also include the methods you used to accomplish the goals and what your role in guiding the client to reach the goal(s) was.

Approach

Give a detailed explanation of the approach to show the client that you have done everything you could to successfully move the client toward goal achievement.

Recommendations

The reaching one goal or a set of goals is often the beginning of a new goal or set of goals, so if there are future opportunities the client should know about, make your recommendations and suggestions in this section. For example, if as a marketing coach, you helped a client design a business website, the recommendations may include suggestions for expanding the website, for growing the readership, or steps to take the website to the next level. If you are a personal training coach that has helped the client lose weight, then your recommendations may include how to maintain his or her goal weight.

Conclusion

The final portion of the report should illustrate what you accomplished and why it was important to illustrate how helping the client to achieve the goal has benefited them.

Post-work communication

When a client relationship ends, this does not signal the conclusion of your relationship with the client. Clients can be sources of repeat business and referral business, so even when your work with a client ends, your communication opportunities with past clients should continue.

Maintaining an up-to-date database of contact information is vital so you can continue to send information to clients. One of the first items you should provide to a client along with their final report — or after the final report — is a survey.

Surveys allow you to gather information and feedback from the client on your service. Good feedback can be used as client testimonials to help you land new business. Poor feedback or constructive criticism can help you to make necessary adjustments to continue to make your coaching business better and better.

Current and past clients are one of the best sources of referrals. Because a client has firsthand experience working with you, when the experience is positive, they can became a raving fan for you. You can make it easy for current and past clients to refer new clients to you by implementing a formal referral program. Referrals can be one of the best routes to take when developing a financially sound business because they are already qualified leads for you.

A formal referral program can offer incentives to clients who send you referrals that turn into clients. Spread the word about your referral program with satisfied clients as relationships draw to an end. You can also send out reminder e-mails or announcements to old clients to rekindle relationships.

COACHING METHODS: DECIDING HOW TO DELIVER YOUR SERVICES

One of the great things about coaching is the various options you have to choose from on how to deliver your coaching services. What is even better is that you are not limited to just one delivery method, so you can interact with clients in multiple ways, and toggle between the methods with each client. Discover the different coaching methods you can use and the pros and cons of using each method to determine the best coaching style for your business:

- Delivery method

- Pros

- Cons

- One-on-one

Some individuals and businesses prefer to work with a coach face-to-face. This is especially true for executive coaches who go into companies and work with managers and executives. Face-to-face meetings build a rapport with clients. Some coaches go into the community with their clients to guide them through real life situations.

Your client-base may be limited based on how much time you have to meet one-on-one and by where your business is located. You may have to set up an office outside of home to provide this kind of service because there may be zoning ordinances in your neighborhood that prevent you from setting up a business in a residential neighborhood.

Workshops and seminars

You can make more money by working with groups of people as opposed to one client at a time. Group coaching also incorporates accountability and group support that does not occur in a one-on-one situation. Group sessions tend to be good sources of one-on-one client work.

You must find a neutral location to meet. There could be a cost associated with renting a location. Scheduling a convenient time to hold group sessions can be complicated and group sessions allow for less time to work on individualized needs.

Online classes and webinars

You can maximize the amount of money you make per hour. You do not need a physical location and clients can work around their schedules. Online sessions also broaden the base of clients. Coaching clients can also post targeting ads and have online forums and discussions in these settings.

You have less of a connection with your clients because you cannot interact face-to-face (unless you are using a Web cam). This makes it harder to create accountability, and this can slow a class down. In some cases, people can log in whenever they like to see lectures and so there is little peer-to-peer interaction or accountability.

Teleconference and teleseminars

The benefits are similar to an online class, but without the need for the Internet. You can meet everyone at once and clients can interact with the coach and with one another.

You may have to buy additional equipment or pay for extra services on your phone line. Teleseminars tend to require a bridge line, which may cost money or limit the amount of attendees on the call.

Choosing the best method of delivery for you

In any journey of discovery, there are adjustments. You have to look ahead to make the decisions needed to reach your goal. Though the pathway may seem to be clear in front of you, you may find that the path to it is not so straight, so you may to make a certain amount of assessment and adjustment needed to become a successful coach. You need to be able to look at how effective your services are and make changes when necessary.

Once you have established your coaching goals, you may still have to make adjustments along the way. You are the one deciding where your destination is and how you intend to get there, so there is not any right destination that works for every coach. You have to decide what is best for you by working within your strengths, so if you work better talking with clients than at writing, then you will work better in one-on-one situations, teleseminars, or phone sessions as opposed to webinars.

With that being said, do not be afraid to try new things by trying new formats or coaching delivery methods. You may discover that you have talents you never imagined.

One-on-one

When the coaching industry first emerged, face-to-face contact was the only delivery method available. An executive coach would go to the company and work individually with executives and managers. For the most part, this is the model many executive coaches still adopt, but phone sessions and Internet interaction are methods more frequently used to hold consultations in lieu of or in addition to providing coaching services in person.

Personal coaches do not tend to hold face-to-face consultations as much as business coaches. Personal coaches tend to rely more on the Internet and telephone for contact. Executive coaches also use telephone contact but face-to-face tends to be more common for group situations.

There are, however, advantages to one-on-one contact. You are able to build more rapport with the client, which fosters an intimate relationship. This is important because the clients must learn to trust a coach before baring his or her soul and talking about what he or she really wants out of life. You can see the client's body language, and you are able to make eye contact, which helps build trust and a deeper level of communication. As an alternative to one-on-one consultations, you can decide to do video chats, which is a meshing of face-to-face contact and Internet chats.

If you do decide to conduct face-to-face sessions with your clients, you will have to choose whether you will meet people in their home, in public, in your office, or your home office. Having an office sets a professional tone, although it can increase the expenses of the business, which can equate to charging clients higher rates, which can lead to losing potential clients to your competitors.

Meeting clients at their work is acceptable if you are an executive coach, but you may not get the same open-door reception if you are a personal coach. If you choose to meet a client at a coffee shop, it may seem more relaxed and less professional, and it lacks the privacy that a closed-door session has. Remember you may be charging clients hundreds of dollars an hour, which seems at odds to chatting over a mocha latte.

Workshops and seminars

Teaching workshops is a way many coaches interact with clients, which permits the coach to work with a group rather than an individual. If you are doing a workshop or seminar at a conference or as a consultant for a company, you may be paid a flat fee, regardless of how many people attend. If you are hosting your own workshop or seminar, however, you can charge a per-person fee, so the more people that attend, the better your profit margin. When you are first starting to develop your reputation, you may even opt to host some free seminars in order to build a client base. Free workshops can be a loss-leader in your business, which means that you are using the free workshop as leverage to up-sell clients into your paid coaching services. One way to accomplish this is to offer discounted sessions to attendees of the workshop as long as they book your services before leaving.

Teaching live workshops and seminars can be more interactive than giving a speech to an audience. Group seminars allow participants to uplift each other. Also, the fact that you are working with a specific group of people, either at a conference or who are from a particular company, allows you, as a coach, to cater your workshop to the specific needs of the attendees.

If you are hosting or working at your first workshop or seminar as a coach to prepare, you will need to conduct some of your own research. You can use a search engine, such as Google, and look for coaching conferences and conventions to see the types of sessions and information being shared. You can also look for workshops and seminars that are industry specific or related to the group you will be working with. For example, if you are a spiritual coach, use words such as:

- Spiritual
- Retreat

- Seminar
- Convention
- Conference
- Soul
- Soul retrieval
- Spirituality
- Spiritual coaching

Online classes, webinars, teleseminars, and teleconferences

If you are running a teleseminar, you can charge each person individually and earn a decent profit, making thousands of dollars each hour rather than a couple of hundred doing individual work with clients. Again, once you have established your following as a one-on-one coach, you can expand your business to coach groups of people, therefore increasing your profit.

Choose a specific topic or area that is of interest to the group you are targeting and be sure to prepare and disseminate any supplemental materials to the participants prior to the class or session. Make sure that you have all of your equipment set up and tested before the appointed hour as well so that you can start and end on time.

You may even opt to increase the number of attendees by joining forces with another professional coach. You can accomplish this in a number of different ways. One is to trade advertising — you promote their webinars and they promote yours. Another way is to collaborate and work together to present an online webinar or class together. Each of you will prepare for your contribution to the class. You then split the cost of advertising and any fees collected. It is a win-win situation. This works well if both of you have particular areas in which you are an expert.

Like workshops and live seminars, online webinars, classes, and teleconferences are great marketing techniques for your one-on-one services. It allows people to sample your services, your style, and your personality. The time and effort you put into these types of seminars are worth money in the bank because it is the best way to get people to notice you and what you have to offer.

Which service delivery format is most comfortable for you and why?

You can try out different service delivery methods to see which ones feel right for you and bring the most profitability to your coaching business. See which methods resonate with you. Consider changing how you deliver your services or trying out new formats. Remember, a happy coach is a successful coach. If you are miserable doing what you are doing, you are doing both you and your clients a disservice. Your unhappiness will begin to show in your service delivery. If you are unhappy doing what you have chosen to do, how do you expect to inspire others?

Some personalities match better with the different types of service delivery already mentioned. Some people are naturally more outgoing than others. Some prefer one-on-one interaction, while others are more content just dealing with people over the Internet. There is no right or wrong way to coach, which is why many coaches use a combination of approaches.

	INTROVERT	EXTROVERT
Characteristics	Quiet, does not like to talk much, prefers reducing coaching to the written word rather than interacting with clients, likes to meet and deal with clients through e-mail, online classes, or forums	Outgoing, life of the party, engaging, likes having people around them and interacting with others on a personal level, enjoys working with people one-on-one
Best Types of Service Delivery	Webinars, online classes, teleseminara, one-on-one (online)	One-on-one (in person); workshops, seminars, teleconferences, teleseminars

MATCHING THE FORMAT
WITH THE CLIENT

Clients are as unique as coaches, so you need to take into consideration that people learn and process information differently. Some need to see something to understand a concept, while others do better when they read about it. These are called learning styles. There are four main types of learners: visual, auditory, reading, and kinesthetic.

For instance, suppose you are working with a client about letting go of the past and the emotional baggage this can sometimes create. There are a number of ways in which you can teach this concept. A good coach is flexible and pays attention to each client's learning style and determines which approach is best for the client.

There are many different models of learning styles, such as the David Kolb model, the Honey and Mumford Learning Styles questionnaire, Anthony

Gregorc's model, and the Sudbury Model of Education. The most common and easiest model to follow, however, is the Neil Fleming's VARK model:

V — Visual

A — Aural/auditory

R — Reading/writing preference

K — Kinesthetic/Tactile

Fleming claimed that visual learners have a preference for seeing, which means they think in terms of pictures and visual aids, such as overhead slides, diagrams, and handouts. Auditory learners best learn through listening to things like lectures, discussions, or tapes. Kinesthetic learners prefer to learn via experience — moving, touching, and doing. Fleming's use in pedagogy allows teachers to prepare classes that address each of these areas. Students can also use the model to identify their learning style and maximize their educational experience by focusing on what benefits them the most.

Visual learners

According to Fleming's methodology, visual learners need to see a coach to benefit from their sessions. They look for body language and facial clues as part of their learning process. These types of learners do better when they have diagrams, books with illustrations, and handouts. These types of learners do not do well watching videos, PowerPoint presentations, or movies in the process of learning.

Visual learners tend to take a lot of notes, because they are able to absorb the information by going through the process of seeing what they are learning by writing it. Visual learners also do well in one-on-one situations when they can see the coach, but also do well with reading materials such as books, eBooks, and articles. They like to see videos and go to workshops, as long as there are visual aids that go along with the lecture.

Auditory learners

Fleming states that auditory learners learn best when they hear what others are saying. They gain information by listening to tone of voice, pitch, and speed, so lectures, talks, forums, and workshops that have a lot of discussion provide the best formats. Auditory learners can understand information from radio and taped materials better than from simply reading books. They need to hear about it to learn it. Seminars, group discussions, and webinars have the greatest impact on learning concepts for this type of client.

As a coach, it is important that you learn these styles because if you are not making a connection with your client, you will find resistance, and eventually your client may quit. It is not the material and guidance that you are providing, but rather the delivery of that material that can be troublesome.

Reading and writing learners

According to Fleming, reading and writing learners are different than visual learners. Though they are using their eyes to gather the information, they use a different part of the brain to process the material. These types of learners learn by reading material, and even writing it. Many strong academic people are reading learners. The focus is on text-based language, both as an input, in the case of reading, and as an output, in the form of writing. These types of learners do well with reading textbooks, research materials, and PowerPoint presentations. They like to read along during a class so printing out your PowerPoint presentation for them to follow can be helpful. They spend a lot of time researching on the Internet, and often have a lot of reference materials close by such as dictionaries and thesauruses.

Kinesthetic learners

In 1987, Neil Fleming and Colleen Mills wrote Not Another Inventory, Rather a Catalyst for Reflection, which was in: To Improve the Academy, Vol. 11, 1992, Page 137. In it, Fleming describes tactile and kinesthetic learners as those who process information through doing — they are experimental learners. They must literally do something to grasp the concept. These types of learners perform well on exercises that are assigned to them, so they tend to thrive in an online class, or through e-mail, as long as you give them something hands-on to do.

These types of learners can be a challenge especially if interacting with them over the phone or the Internet because it requires more creativity on the part of the coach. Role-playing really helps with this type of learning, which is where you take on the roles of people in a certain situations. You can even switch roles of client and coach to teach a point as well. The more they can experience the lesson, the easier it is for them to grasp.

If they are in a group-learning situation, it is better if you use real life examples with them rather than a lot of abstract theories and lessons. Give them situations or pictures that illustrate a situation that they may be facing and have them create a solution or describe what is going on.

You will need to reduce the amount of notes or papers you give to them, because not only will these not be as effective, but they can sometimes overwhelm the tactile learner. Pairing them with other clients works well, especially if you can do problem solving together.

Multimodal learners

You will find that many clients are a mix of styles and will use one style over another depending on the information that is to be learned and the learning environment. Fleming suggests that more than 60 percent of the population is multimodal. This should not distress you as a coach because it gives you more options. If you find that one approach is not working with a particular client, you can slip into a different one. You might also find that multimodal learners will switch into different modes themselves to grasp a particular concept. This is often a subconscious one, but the astute coach can recognize the shift and change their delivery accordingly. Coaching is an active profession in which the coach must be alert to the needs of their client at all times.

How to determine a client's learning style

So, how do you know what type of person you are dealing with in your coaching business? You can send your clients online to the VARK site, run by Neil Fleming, at **www.vark-learn.com** or search the Internet for similar tests to assess a person's learning style. The results will give you an idea of the client's learning style and help guide you to which method of delivery will be most effective for the client. It may only be worth your time to determine the learning style of one-on-one clients — you may not have the time to do this for everyone taking your online class and still be able to completely change how you are presenting your material. Plus, with group coaching, your goal is to appeal to a broad variety of clients.

Thus, your group setting, such as a class or workshop, will have clients with all three learning styles. Because of this, it is important to consider adding components to your lessons and classes that incorporate all of the learning styles.

For instance, suppose you have a lesson for an online class full of executive coaching clients about how to get the maximum efficiency out of your employees. In the lesson, you can include handouts that describe why this is important and ways your clients can improve their skills when dealing with their employees. This covers the visual learner, because you have given them something to read. You can also include graphs and illustrations to support certain points in the text.

Next, you can include a broadcast of a radio show that covered this same topic. You have now given something to the auditory learners. Finally, you can include exercises that clients can do over the week to try out the techniques that are mentioned in the lesson, and require them to report their results. This covers the kinesthetic learners, and by reporting back you have included the visual and auditory learners as well, as they are encouraged to record, understand, and reiterate their results.

You can also assume that people have a sense of what type of learners they are. They will be attracted to certain types of services. You can assume that those who read your blog are primarily visual learners, while those who you see at your lectures are auditory or visual learners. Those seeking one-on-one interaction can be any of these types of learners, which is why it is more important to explore which learning styles work for these clients early on.

If you include different delivery modalities of your information, you should not only be able to assure that your message is being understood better, but you will also increase your chances of helping your clients change their lives. And, with more successful clients singing your praises, you will ultimately increase the number of clients you will attract.

CHECKLIST

✓ Understand how to interact with clients at different parts during the project.

✓ Survey customers to gather feedback on your service.

✓ Implement a referral program.

Chapter 12:
Building and Growing
Your Business

In this chapter, you will:

- Learn how to build credibility and create passive income.

- How to create a team of experts to help you in your business.

- Learn how to handle moving or upgrading your office location, or establishing an office that was once home-based.

- Discover how to juggle multiple client projects at one time.

As you continue to work as a coach, you will start to gain momentum. You will gather more and more clients. You will probably work for some of your clients on more than one goal. Some of your clients will send new clients your way through referrals. All of these activities help to build your business. Some coaches choose to keep their business small and continue to run it out of their home on their own. Other coaches take on enough business to require additional coaches, along with administrative and marketing help. Some coaching businesses even transform into multi-million dollar corporations. You can grow your business from a small coaching firm to a bigger one by expanding your client base. In some cases, you create additional business without taking on any more coaching clients by becoming an information mogul.

INFORMATIONAL PRODUCTS

Coaches are essentially information moguls because their service involves sharing their expertise and information with their clients to solve problems. This means there are several ways coaches can build credibility and generate passive income simultaneously. Some of the options for creating passive income include:

Live workshops and seminars

If you cater to a local audience or want to invite people from different areas to one location, you can sell entrance tickets to live workshops and seminars. You can use these live events to share valuable information with your audience. Live events are also great places to sell your other products and services and to gather qualified leads to up-sell at a later date. Be sure to implement a system where you can collect names and contact information for attendees. Run a contest or offer a drawing prize as a way to gather this information.

Webinars

Webinars are online versions of live workshops and seminars. webinars allow you to broaden your audience to anyone in the world that has a computer with Internet access. Some coaches use a free webinar as a lead-in to attract an audience and then up-sell the attendees on another product or service with a strong call to action at the end of the webinar.

Teleseminars

Teleseminars are similar to webinars, but as the name suggests, they are conducted over the phone. Attendees call a number and use a pass code that you provide to them, and then they use this information to get on the line at the scheduled time.

Keynote speaking at conferences and other speaking engagements: Conferences, associations, and other groups are always on the hunt for good speakers. If you can get in front of a room of your target audience at one of these events, this is a great way for you to build credibility. These are also prime locations for selling your other products and services.

Write and sell a book

Experts write books, so picking a hot topic in your industry that you can shine the light on or share your expert advice on can become a book. You may be able to shop the book for publishing, but you also have the option to self-publish the book to get it to market faster and easier.

Sell informational products such as CDs, audio files, e-books, and workbooks

You can record your teleseminars, webinars, and speaking engagements and sell these items online or at your engagements. That is the best part about something like a teleseminar or e-book — you can prepare it one time and sell it many times over.

Since these informational products are created once and can be sold over and over again, this is a great way to accomplish both goals — building credibility with your audience, and generating passive income.

CREATING A TEAM

The ability to delegate is one of the prime characteristics of a leader. Though many coaches start off as a one-man show to keep costs down until they can get the business to turn a profit, other coaches see the benefit of turning a profit faster by delegating duties to others sooner rather than later.

At some point in running your business, you will come to a crossroads where you are overwhelmed with work and need help. The degree of help you require can vary from coach to coach; it may simply be that you need help with administrative tasks, or you may need help in additional areas such as marketing, accounting, and graphic design.

You have two options for obtaining the assistance you need. You can either hire employees on a full-time or part-time basis, or you can outsource your needs to freelancers or businesses that can fill the role. If the coaching aspect of your business is more than you can handle, there may even come a time when you need to hire an additional coach or two. Which route you take may be strictly for financial reasons. If you hire full-time or part-time employees, there are salaries and benefits that may become expensive for you to cover. You may also have to provide a place for them to work with a desk, computer, and phone line. Outsourcing and hiring freelancers, on the other hand, allows you to get the help you need without these added expenses. Typically, you are only responsible for paying them for the work they complete for you.

Finding employees or individuals to outsource the work to can be a complex project because first you have to find qualified candidates, conduct interviews, and then finally narrow down your options until you hire someone. Career and job websites such as Monster (**www.monster.com**), CareerBuilder (**www.careerbuilder.com**), and Yahoo!® HotJobs (**www.**

hotjobs.yahoo.com) allow you to post open positions in your company for a fee. You can also use free classified websites such as Craigslist, Kijiji, and BackPage.

Spend some time spreading the word with customers and colleagues about the type of people you are looking to add to your team. Some of the best employees can be found through people you know and people who know you and your business.

HOW TO MOVE YOUR OFFICE

If and when it comes to a point where your coaching business outgrows your home office, you will have to find office space to rent. Typically, upgrading your office occurs because you hire on employees that need to come into the office to work; therefore, you need space to house them. Coaches that start to work more on a face-to-face basis where clients come to their office typically need a professional office that is not in their home to conduct these meetings. Other coaches have personal situations with their home office that propel them to separate their work life from their home life, so they need to find an office and start the process of setting the office up.

Revisit Chapter 3 of this book for in-depth details on finding and setting up an office space that works for your business. Moving an office can be a stressful event, but there are ways you can reduce the pressure moving can put on your business. First, make sure that you think of every detail involved in the move. For example, pick a move date and time that is as unobtrusive to your business as possible. If you normally work during the week, then use a weekend to make the move.

Prepare the new office ahead of time by having phone lines and computer networks installed before the old office phone lines and Internet access are switched or turned off. This allows you time to troubleshoot without missing calls or e-mails. It is also imperative that you prepare your clients for the move before it happens. When you meet with clients in the time leading up to the move, let them know that you are getting ready to move your office in case they have trouble getting in touch with you. Send out an e-mail reminder to clients and the rest of your subscriber list to make them aware of the situation. You and any other company employees should also put an automatic response on your e-mails saying that you are in the process of moving the business. Voicemail greetings should also share this information with callers.

One of the biggest shocks that home-based coaches feel when they upgrade into an office location is the financial stretch. Going from paying zero rent to paying what may equate to thousands of dollars in rent each month is something you have to mentally prepare yourself to handle. On top of the operating expenses of the business, you will most likely need at least one employee to run the office when you are not there. This need adds the cost of paying a wage or salary, and maybe even benefits to cover the employee.

Conclusion

Now you have it: You have all of the tools and know-how needed to become a successful coach. No matter what has influenced your move — a desire to be a business owner, being laid off from your job, being forced into early retirement, or seeking a more lucrative career move for you and your family — you now know how to resolve and overcome the challenges and obstacles of becoming a coach.

Coaching work offers a rewarding experience where you sit in the driver's seat of your career and financial future. Making your own schedule, making your own decisions, and helping clients will empower you. Showcase your expertise by pulling answers from your own knowledge and experience, and then use this information to apply a solution to a client's problem.

It is not that you lack the knowledge to be a coach. It is about combining your area of expertise with your ability to run a successful business. If you use this book as your guide, you are halfway there; now it is up to you to take the necessary steps to make your dream a reality. Keep this book with you as a reference as you work on putting your business together or when facing a challenge in your business; you will be able to use it for years to come.

Appendix: Coaching Schools and Organizations

International Coaching Federation (ICF) offers accreditation to coaching schools as well as membership, networking, and an annual conference.

Life Coach Institute offers a 30-day online program for life coaches and an option for life coach certification.

The Life Coach Information Forum (www.lifecoachinformationforum. com) offers a coach certification program of 350 training hours over an eight-month period. It also offers a coach support network where you can interact with other coaches. It is accredited by the ICF and also offers public events and training opportunities.

International Coaching Bureau (www.coachinginternationally.org) provides accreditation to coaches and coaching schools and a free annual coaching summit.

Certified Coaches Alliance (www.certifiedcoachesalliance.com/index1. htm) provides a list of schools and an accreditation program.

Coaches Training Institute (www.thecoaches.com/coach-training) offers a number of graduate programs and certification.

Coach U (www.coachinc.com/CoachU) offers The Advanced Coaching Program™ (ACP™), which meets the academic requirements for becoming an Associate Certified Coach (ACC), Professional Certified Coach (PCC) or Master Certified Coach (MCC) through the International Coach Federation (ICF).

Bibliography

Anderson, M. *Executive Briefing: Case Study on the Return on Investment of Executive Coaching*. Metrixglobal, 2005.

Brown-Volkman, D. *Four Steps to Building , A Profitable Coaching Practice*. Lincoln, NE: iUniverse. 2003.

Coachville.com. *The Coaching Starter Kit*. New York, NY: W.W. Norton and Company. 2003.

Fairley, S. & Shout, C. *Getting Started in Personal and Executive Coaching*. San Francisco, CA: John Wiley & Sons. 2004.

Flaherty, J. *Coaching:Evoking Excellence in Others*. Boston:Elsevier, 2005.

Grodzki, L. & Allen, W. *The Business and Practice of Coaching*. New York, NY: W.W. Norton and Company. 2005.

O'Neill, M. *Executive Coaching with Backbone and Heart. 2nd ed.*, San Francisco, CA: John Wiley & Sons. 2007.

Pinson, L. & Jinnett, J. *Steps to Small Business Start Up, Everything You Need to Know to Turn Your Idea into a Successful Business.* Chicago:Kaplan, 2006.

Sitarz, D. *Sole Proprietorship, Small Business Start Up Kit. 2nd Ed.* Carbondale: Nova, 2007.

Starr, J *The Coaching Manual, the definitive guide to the process, principles and skills of personal coaching.* Great Britain; Pearson Education Limited. 2003.

Whitworth, L. , Kimsey-House, K., Kimsey-House, H., Sandahl, P. *Co-Active Coaching. 2nd ed.*, Mountain View, CA: Davies-Black. 2007.

http://www.myownbusiness.org/business_permits_license/

http://www.entrepreneur.com/startingabusiness/startupbasics/namingyourbusiness/article76958.html

http://www.inc.com/articles/1998/03/13058.html

http://www.essortment.com/career/bookkeepingbasi_sald.htm

Author Biographies

Kristie Lorette has been a content writer and marketing professional for the last 14 years, which has allowed her the opportunity to write copy for and create collateral such as brochures, newsletters, articles, press releases, advertisements, websites, and other content writing. She has a Bachelor of Science degree in marketing and multinational business from Florida State University, as well as a Master of Business Administration from Nova Southeastern University.

Lorette is also a freelance copywriter and marketing consultant, specializing in the financial services, mortgage, real estate, event planning, museum, green living, and non-profit industries. She has had hands-on experience in of these all industries. Lorette can be contacted directly at kristie@studiokwriting.com for all copywriting and marketing needs. She offers nationwide service, with local service in the Miami metro area. For more information about Lorette's experience vist her website, **www. studiokwriting.com**.

John N Peragine, Ph.D., is a freelance writer and classical musician. John holds a B.S. in psychology from Appalachian State University. This is John's fourth book. He loves to hike and spend time with his children. When John is not writing, he plays the piccolo with the Western Piedmont Symphony.

Index